Praise for
SHIFT WORK

"*Shift Work* is more than just a sports book. Tie tells about his personal and professional life, from being a young boy to the present. The book is a winner, just like Tie."

—Don Cherry

"Tie is a loyal friend who is one of a kind on and off the ice. The best teammate I never had."

—Mario Lemieux

"Without Tie at my side, I couldn't have accomplished what I did in Toronto."

—Mats Sundin

"Tie and I have many things in common—first and most obvious being our extremely large head sizes. But what is most endearing and special about Tie is the size of his heart, his sense of humor, and his amazing generosity. I love him like a brother. My four beautiful children all refer to him as Uncle Pumpkin—see if you can figure out why."

—Mark Wahlberg

"I loved *Shift Work*. It is a must read for anyone who is passionate about hockey, as I am. But what makes the book particularly memorable is the telling of Tie's remarkable life both on and off the ice. He is a real and inspiring champ at everything he does. I am very proud to call Tie my friend."

Peltz

T0025989

"With Tie, what you see is what you get. And there is a world shortage of that, in every respect. Tie is the baseline for 'real,' and he is 'old school.'"

—Mitch Goldhar

"I learned something about Tie when we were both young and playing for the Rangers, and it is still true to this day: there's no challenge he isn't willing to take on. I'm talking about life, business, you name it. He takes on all of his challenges head on."

—Adam Graves

"Tie Domi was always driven at what he did. People that are driven at certain things—and I only saw the hockey side—you know it is going to translate off the ice. It just has to; it is part of their DNA and part of their character . . .Tie would be a really good example of that."

—Glenn Healy

"*Shift Work* is a story of true grit and is sure to inspire people who have followed Tie's career on and off the ice. Throughout our long friendship, I've seen firsthand Tie's dedication to family, loyalty to friends, and humility and generous spirit towards his many fans."

—Mark Silver

"Tie Domi is one of the most loyal friends that you could ever ask to be a part of your life. I really got to know Tie when I coached his son, Max, who played with my son, Eric. Most people see Tie as the best protector of the stars he played with. I see him as a man who has a bigger heart than his head—a man who will always be there for all his friends. With all that said, his greatest asset is his family. I have been around many people, but nobody loves their children the way Tie loves Carlin, Avery, and Max. He is the best family man I have ever met. I love Tie Domi."

—Bill Comrie

"Tie sets his mind to a goal and he does it. That's the way he did it in hockey. You want to be his friend; you want to be close to him. You feel secure when you're next to him, not only because of the physical aspect that nobody is going to mess with you but because he's a true friend.

—Bob Kaiser

"The book is an entertaining, fast-paced read that . . . pulls back the curtain on his career."

—*The Hockey News*

"The book . . . puts it all in context, to explain where he'd come from, the values his blue-collar immigrant parents instilled and which he's attempted to teach his own three children."

—*Toronto Star*

"There is more to Domi than a flurry of fists . . . When it comes to Tie Domi, there's never a dull moment."

—*The Globe and Mail*

SHIFT WORK

TIE DOMI

WITH JIM LANG

Published by Simon & Schuster

New York   London   Toronto   Sydney   New Delhi

SIMON &
SCHUSTER
CANADA

Simon & Schuster Canada
A Division of Simon & Schuster, Inc.
166 King Street East, Suite 300
Toronto, Ontario M5A 1J3

Copyright © 2015 by TD International

Reasonable efforts have been made to contact copyright holders for permission and to give credit. If additional information is provided, changes may be made to future printings.

All rights reserved, including the right to reproduce this book or portions thereof in any form whatsoever. For information, address Simon & Schuster Canada Subsidiary Rights Department, 166 King Street East, Suite 300, Toronto, Ontario, M5A 1J3.

This Simon & Schuster Canada edition October 2016

SIMON & SCHUSTER CANADA and colophon are registered trademarks of Simon & Schuster, Inc.

For information about special discounts for bulk purchases, please contact Simon & Schuster Special Sales at 1-800-268-3216 or CustomerService@simonandschuster.ca.

Library and Archives Canada Cataloguing in Publication

Domi, Tie, 1969–, author Shift work / Tie Domi; with Jim Lang
1. Domi, Tie, 1969–. 2. Hockey players—Canada—Biography.
3. National Hockey League—Biography. I. Lang, Jim, 1965–, author. II. Title.
GV848.5.D64A3 2016
796.962092
C2016-901486-X

Manufactured in the United States of America

5 7 9 10 8 6

ISBN 978-1-4767-8250-8
ISBN 978-1-4767-8251-5 (pbk)
ISBN 978-1-4767-8252-2 (ebook)

CONTENTS

For my dad

For my dad

SHIFT WORK

INTRODUCTION

I T WAS January 14, 1992, and I felt like I was on top of the world as I walked into Madison Square Garden. I was only twenty-two years old, but I was getting ready to play another game in what was already my second season with the New York Rangers.

The day had started off no differently than any other up to that point in my career. I got up, and the first thing I did was pour myself a bowl of Frosted Flakes. Some days I would add some chopped-up banana, but not that morning—just a bowl of Frosted Flakes to fuel me up before heading off to the rink for the morning skate.

I always sat in the corner of the dressing room at MSG. Nobody was on my left. James Patrick—one of the Rangers' more experienced defencemen and the sweetest guy ever—and I sat beside each other every practice, but on game nights it was always a different guy on my right side. The trainers and equipment managers would bring our skates, gloves, and sticks in for games at MSG from our practice rink, but no matter who was beside me, game after game, I always had that corner stall.

INTRODUCTION

At morning practices, James and the older guys on the team always wanted to hear my stories from the night before. James was in his usual good mood, and as soon as I sat down, they were asking me for my stories. When I was young, I wasn't a big drinker, but we did have a lot of fun back then, and I got a kick out of making people laugh. The older guys—married ones, especially—would want to hear what I'd been up to the night before.

After the morning skate, I headed to the hotel across from MSG for my usual pregame meal: two big bowls of pasta with chicken breasts and some bread to carb up for the game. For dessert, I always had vanilla ice cream with chocolate sauce.

After I'd stuffed myself full of pasta, I usually tried lying down for a pregame nap. I am really not a good sleeper—never have been. And on a game day I could never rest all that much. My whole career, I was never afraid of anybody. But in the afternoon of every game day, I would find myself curled up in a ball on my bed, wide awake. I assumed it was my nerves. I was confused because I knew that I shouldn't be nervous about anything. I wasn't afraid of what I had to do, but still, there I would be most afternoons, curled up in a ball and unable to sleep. It was only years later, when I turned forty, that I found out I have a gluten intolerance. And here I was, stuffing myself with big bowls of pasta day after day. No wonder I was in so much discomfort.

Like I did most game days, I eventually gave up on getting a good nap and decided to make my way to the rink. On game nights I spent as little time at the rink as possible before the game. I would be the last guy to get there and the last to leave. Walking down the hallway to the dressing room, just like every other night, I said hello to everyone in the building. But there was one person who stood out among everyone else. One of my newest teammates just happened to be one of the game's all-time greats: Mark Messier. He'd joined the team a few months earlier. As I passed by him doctoring up his sticks on my way into the dressing room, my energy level kicked up a notch.

Getting prepared for a game was a little different for me than it was for everyone else. The other guys would be thinking that they had to stop this or that guy, or that they had to keep the puck out of the net, or that they needed to score. I had to get in a mindset where I would be ready to react at any given time if an opponent took advantage of any of my teammates. I always had to be prepared to drop my gloves and do my job. That's just the way it was, and it's why I never started getting dressed until ten minutes before warm-up— I didn't want to sit in the dressing room and think about fighting.

When that ten-minute mark hit, I finally started getting ready. Before I put my gear on, I jumped into my usual cold shower. As soon as the freezing water hit me, I felt myself sink into that familiar zone. The switch went on in my head and I realized what I might have to do that night. Afterward, I stepped back into the locker room and put on my equipment. No special taping or sharpening; I liked to keep things simple and straightforward.

As I laced up my skates, I looked over to see what the other guys were doing. Some of them had cups of coffee in their hands. When I was young, I never understood that habit. As an older player I drank coffee, but not when I was young and had just started playing. Back then, I didn't need anything except the opportunity to do something I love. This being the 1990s, some of those same guys swilling coffee also had cigarettes sticking out of their mouths. The league was a lot different back then.

The start of the anthem always made me even more focused. Like I did before every game, I said my usual quick prayer for my dad and grandmother after the anthem, and then crammed my helmet back on my head. Game time.

It wasn't long after the puck dropped that I realized this was going to be a special night: in the first period, I scored. That night, I was playing with Tim Kerr and John Ogrodnick, and I was lucky to even be on that line. Kerr was playing centre, and Ogrodnick was on the left wing, and both of them were fifty-goal scorers at some point in their careers. Those guys helped me get my confidence up—their nickname for me was "Little Brother." It felt good playing with them. They loved it, too, because they knew nobody was going to hit them. When I got on their line, they suddenly had a lot more room than usual to work with.

And that night in particular, in the first period, we made it count. I broke out into the neutral zone on the left wing with Kerr carrying the puck up the middle and Ogrodnick cutting across the Buffalo Sabres' blue line. Kerr fed me the puck as I burst ahead, and as I crossed the blue line, I dropped a pass back to him and got a step on the Sabres' defenceman as I cut towards the net. When Kerr reached the top of the circle, he ripped a wrist shot on net. Clint Malarchuk, the Sabres' goalie, made a good pad save, but the puck bounced out in front of the crease. We'd caught the Sabres' defence on a bad change, so when I saw that puck just sitting there, I zeroed in on it. I flew down the left wing in the clear, and before Malarchuk could get back in position, I snapped the puck under his left side into the back of the net.

And like I had done once before in my career, when I scored that night at Madison Square Garden, I rode my stick down centre ice to celebrate, just like Tiger Williams used to do with the Toronto Maple Leafs in the 1970s. Because I thought that's what I was supposed to do. Not only that, but this was only the second goal of my career! So when I beat Malarchuk, I was pretty excited, and it didn't take much convincing to get me to celebrate.

Later in the game, during the second period, I fought Gord Donnelly. I had fought Donnelly two nights earlier in Buffalo in a game that the Sabres won. The only difference this night was that we were the ones who were winning. When the dust settled, it was clear I had gotten the better of him. Even though he was a lot bigger than me, I tagged him with a couple of good lefts at the end of the fight just before the linesmen stepped in. Because Donnelly and I had fought just two days before, I knew exactly how to beat him. I could see his fighting style in my mind, and because I could read him, I could pick the precise spots when I could nail him with those lefts. After the fight, I felt so good that I started showboating and playing to the crowd as I skated to the penalty box. I mimed punching a speed bag, and I was laughing all the way to the box. The crowd was in a frenzy.

When the game ended, not only had we beaten the Sabres 6–2, but I had scored a goal and done my job standing up for my team. To top it all off, I was named the third star of the game. Messier had had a four-point night and the Rangers fans were loving us, but as I skated off the ice, it was my name that the packed crowd at the Garden was chanting. I didn't think it was possible to feel any better about myself than I did at that moment. It was a great night to be in New York at MSG. I felt pretty good about myself; I thought I had it all figured out.

Well, that feeling didn't last very long.

Moments after I got off the ice, Messier said, "Tie, come here," and led me into the trainer's room away from the rest of the team. It wasn't the biggest trainer's room at the old Garden, and as Messier shut the door, I knew he was serious, so I immediately calmed down and focused. He turned to face me with a serious look in his eye.

The first thing Messier said to me was, "Enough is enough." He told me that I had to stop the WWE antics and the showboating after fights. He looked me right in the eyes, and he said that I had to change my ways. "You're *never* going to get respect in this league if you don't respect your peers!" he said.

I remember that I didn't say a word; for the first time in my life, I just listened. Like every guy in the league, I knew that Messier's track record spoke for itself. With five Stanley Cups, a Conn Smythe Trophy, a Hart Memorial Trophy, and over a thousand points, Messier was known as one of the greatest leaders in all professional sports, ever. Messier continued to school me. He did all the talking, and I just stood there and nodded my head. There wasn't much I could say as the master told the kid what it takes to be a pro in the NHL. When Messier finished, I just said, "Thank you."

Looking back, I think Messier knew exactly how to handle me. He knew that I was fearless. I wasn't the best player on the team. And I wasn't the captain. I wasn't a bad teammate, because we all have our own ways. But I did need a reality check. Messier pulled me aside because he saw something in me. I think he knew and believed that I could be more than a fighter. When I got to play, I usually did pretty well. I just didn't get the opportunity very often.

Just like I was, Messier was a big believer in treating everybody on the team like family and in keeping them close. Messier thought that if everyone was a part of the team and was pulling their weight, then we had a better chance at winning. And Messier was all about winning. That was another reason why I listened to him so closely—because I was the same way: I just wanted to win.

INTRODUCTION

I honestly never cared about stats; I only cared about winning. I have been that way since I was a kid.

As I was listening to Messier in that trainer's room, it hit me that I had a lot to learn about the NHL. More than anything, I realized that respect was something I would need to earn in the big leagues. When Messier pulled me into that trainer's room in New York and said, "You're *never* going to get respect in this league if you don't respect your peers!" it changed my career. It changed my life. That moment in time and those words changed everything for me and stayed with me even after the end of my time in the NHL.

I was in a daze as I walked back to the dressing room. I took off my gear quietly at my locker. As I was putting on my clothes, Messier reappeared beside me and said, "Where are we going? Let's go for a drink."

And this was just minutes after he chewed me out! I was shocked. One minute Messier was shredding me, and then a half hour later, he's asking me where we're going. I realized right then that he really cared about me and that he was just trying to help me. So I did what anyone else would have done. I went for a drink with Messier. And when we went out afterwards, it was like nothing had ever happened. Messier never even brought up our conversation. That's the way he was, and that is why he was such a great leader. Once a thing was done, it was done and it was time to move on, and he never embarrassed you about it or brought it up in front of anyone else.

The funny thing about that night in New York is that it basically sums up my entire life. Every time I have been taught a lesson or run into hard times, I have made sure that I learned from those moments and bounced back. We all need a push in the right direction sometimes. The important thing is to be humble enough to take that advice to heart. Nowadays, I like to refer to stuff like that as "old school" values. Others might just call it common sense.

When Messier pulled me aside, I didn't sulk about it. I listened to him and did what he said. I realized I would have to be accountable for my actions and change my ways. There is no shame in falling down or having someone in a leadership role pull you aside and tell you that you are doing something wrong. The real shame is if you don't listen to them.

At the end of the day, what Messier told me that night really wasn't too complicated. He just made me tone it down and respect my peers more. The timing of his talk could not have been more perfect. I was in my early twenties, and that night I told myself that I would try to do things the right way for the rest of my career.

Turns out I still had a long way to go.

1

Beginnings

Beginnings

M Y STORY doesn't begin with me. It begins with my parents. Growing up in Albania, my dad, John Domi, experienced a lot of hardship, both during World War II and after the war, under the communists. While my sister, brother, and I were growing up, one of the earliest stories we remember being told was about the time that my father was shot in the head while he was fleeing Albania. For the rest of my dad's life, long after the wound healed, the bullet fragment stayed lodged in his forehead. I guess there was a piece that the doctors weren't able to remove, and so it was just left there until the day he died. It was on the outer part of his left eyebrow, and when you touched the spot, you could feel the bullet fragment; it was like a small rock stuck under his skin.

I can't count the number of times we heard that story when we were kids. Every time we felt for the bullet, we heard it told again. But I'm not sure my brother, sister, or I ever understood the reality of it. As we listened to the story, we sat in our living room, on our dad's lap, with the comforts of a good home and a nice family. His stories of tough times and the war were, to us, just that—a bunch of stories. Dash and Trish and I were all born in Canada. We didn't know anything about war or what it was like to be shot at. We were more worried about the kinds of things most kids are worried about: school, our friends, or what sport we would play next.

My dad's struggles only began with the war. His life in Albania and his journey to make a better life for himself and his family were ordeals in and of themselves. Following the war, the communists in Albania—who had led the resistance against the Italians and the Nazis—became the main military and political power in the country. After Albania had been liberated from the Nazis, it officially became a communist country and changed its name to the People's Republic of Albania. The communist regime that then followed was nasty. My dad was completely anticommunist. He remembered how anyone caught practising any kind of religion would be arrested, tortured, and even killed. Albania eventually became part of the Soviet Union's communist bloc, and my dad could only see life getting more difficult because of it. Albania was not a good place to be living in the late 1940s and early 1950s.

Not everyone was happy with where the country was headed. There were lots of people who served in the anticommunist movement, but in reality, many of them were actually spies for the communists. My father and his brother were in the same unit working against the Communist Party. But their unit had been infiltrated by a group of these spies, so all of their activities were being reported to the communist powers that had taken over the country. I am not sure exactly when or how my father and uncle realized they were in trouble, but it was clear that they were at risk, and so, in 1950, they decided they had to get out of the country immediately.

At that time, Albania was one of the hardest countries in the world to enter or exit. So just getting out was an incredible challenge. But it was even more difficult for my dad and my uncle—because their anticommunist past had been reported, they had to avoid any official exits. That meant they would have to sneak across the border. It took my dad and uncle a long time to get out of the country. They moved only by foot or car, and only at night. During the daylight, they would hide out with sympathetic Albanian families in their barns or basements. They were smart and lucky, and eventually they made their way to the border of what was then Yugoslavia, which they finally ended up crossing in the middle of the night.

After escaping, my dad found himself in a town called Pristina, part of present-day Kosovo. It was there that he met my mom, Meyrem, in 1954. It didn't take long for my dad to promise my mom that he would marry her, but neither one of them expected that to take as long as it did. Things got even more complicated when my mom and her family immigrated to Turkey. My grandmother on my mom's side was Albanian and my grandfather was Turkish, and they would switch between languages whenever they felt like it. Luckily, my dad could keep up—he spoke seven languages. But he couldn't travel to Turkey with my mom and her family, so he ended up bouncing through Austria, Germany, and Italy, trying to find the right country to settle his new family in. Dad ended up spending time in seven countries before deciding that Canada was the place for him.

My dad finally arrived in Canada in 1963. When he first got there, he settled in Winnipeg and worked for a time for the Canadian Pacific Railway; it was common for new immigrants to work on the railway. After a lonely year of working out west and saving money, my dad moved to Toronto, where he worked for Cara Foods, loading supplies onto planes at the airport. Finally, nine years after they had met in Pristina, my dad managed to scrape together enough savings to bring my mom over to join him in Canada.

I can't even imagine how tough it must have been for my mom when she settled in Canada. She was in a strange country and she didn't speak a word of English. But she and my dad had each other, and in May 1965, a year after my mom arrived in Canada, my brother, Dash, was born. When my mom gave birth to Dash, she didn't know a single person in Canada other than my dad, and she felt incredibly lonely in the hospital as she watched the woman next to her receive flowers and visitors. But then, one day, a woman arrived with flowers not for the other person in the room, but for my mom. This woman came over and actually introduced herself in Albanian. It turns out that my father had met the woman's husband while frequenting a coffee shop where he met with other Albanian men. He told them that he and my mom had a new baby boy, and they all knew my mother was new to the country. So this woman's husband had come home and suggested that his wife go to visit my mom, and she did. From that moment on, they were best friends for life. Suddenly, my parents had a whole new connection to their new home, and their community began to grow.

It was about this time, when Dash was a baby and my dad was still working at Cara Foods, that Dad took a trip to Windsor, Ontario, where he heard some other Albanians had settled. Nobody in our family had ever been to Windsor or the surrounding area before. The only thing they knew was that there were some Albanians living there. My dad got to know some of the people from that network, and so, once he got to Windsor, he discovered that the people he was supposed to meet actually lived outside of Windsor, in a town called Belle River. He arrived there and found that the family he was supposed to meet owned a restaurant. And that restaurant just happened to be up for sale.

All of a sudden, my dad loved the idea of living in Belle River and running that restaurant. As a place to raise a family, Belle River was a good spot. There weren't many people living there— maybe 3,500 at the time—and it was a tight-knit community with a large number of French-Canadian families. Above all else, it was a very safe little town. Back in those days, nobody locked their front doors. And after what my mom and dad had gone through their whole lives, a nice, small, safe town was just what they were looking for.

Using whatever savings he had, and partnering with another Albanian family friend, my father was able to buy the restaurant. It was called Edna's Lunch, named after the cook and owner. At the same time, my parents moved into a nice little house. It was an orange brick bungalow with a big backyard. When my sister, Trish, was born, she had her own room. And when I came along, I got to share a bunk bed with Dash. The house had a basement, where we would play, but only in the daytime—my sister thought there were Martians that came out at night. Much as we loved playing there, we spent just as much—if not more—of our childhood at Edna's. It was like our second home. We could always swing by to have a hamburger (still the best I've ever had), bring our friends to eat, make our own milk shakes, play the jukebox, do the dishes for twenty-five cents (which was a lot for a kid back then), serve from behind the coffee counter, work the cash register (which was cool when you're a kid), play tag, and drive the employees crazy.

Because we spent so much time outside our home, we weren't just raised by our dad and mom. My dad had made a promise to my mom when they were young that they would bring every single one of their family members over to Canada. Everything they did and every hour they worked was all for that. My dad was the driving force that kept that going, and eventually, he and my mom were able to bring over a number of their relatives, including my mom's mother, two of her brothers, and two of her sisters. My grandmother even lived with us for a time. In the world I come from, family stays with family, and there's always room for one more. It was important to my parents to never forget or let go of their connection to the lives they'd had to leave behind in Albania. When I was born, my parents had given me the traditionally Albanian name Tahir, and for the first few years of my life, I went by that. But my name quickly changed when I started school. For some reason, my kindergarten teacher started calling me Tie, and it stuck. Before long, even my mom was calling me Tie. Still, with so much family starting to gather around us, we never forgot where we'd come from, and my immediate family learned to always stick together.

As I grew up, my dad did well with Edna's, and so he started buying a number of other properties across the street. He eventually bought a pizza place, another restaurant, a couple of Laundromats, and a variety store. Of course, with so many businesses to run at once, my father was always at work. I'm not sure why he was always working; maybe it was an old-country Albanian thing. Whatever the reason, we simply didn't know any better. We thought that's the way it was supposed to be: a dad was supposed to work all the time to provide for his family.

And my mom's work ethic was no different. She was a typical, old-school European mother. She kept the house spotless—you couldn't help but take your shoes off when you walked in, it was so clean. Laundry had to be ironed and folded perfectly, right down to the underwear. There were fresh sheets on the bed every day. My mom spoiled us at home. On top of that, she cooked for an army every day. Friends and family were constantly coming and going, and they always knew my mom would have a ton of food ready.

But as hard as my family worked during the week, we always tried to have a little fun on the weekends. Every now and then, we would get together with family and friends, with all the kids playing games like hide-and-go-seek or kick-the-can together. It was a classic Albanian scene: all the mothers preparing a meal and talking together while the men played cards and argued about politics. At these sorts of get-togethers, my dad was the only father who would take the time to see what the kids were doing and goof around with us. All of the kids loved him. To this day, a lot of our cousins have favourite stories about my dad. My dad took care of people. He was a loyal man, the kind of person we always wanted to be around. He was constantly cracking jokes to make us laugh, and he woke up and went to bed every day with a smile on his face. He did what so many people struggle to do: he came to Canada with nothing and built a good life for his family. To us, that was something to treasure.

Because my dad's work took him all over the place, and with all of the sports my brother, sister, and I were playing, everyone in my family had different hours. We were constantly arriving home at different times of the day, so we didn't have any set mealtimes; my mom would just feed us as we got home. Thanks to all of my dad's hard work, we weren't poor. But that being said, we didn't have much extra, either. Of course, we didn't know any better at the time. We had a decent house, plenty to eat, and clothes on our back. We played sports and had fun. What else did we really need? Despite that, my dad never let us forget how hard he and my mom had to work for it all. When we were young, he would tell us stories that most immigrant children have heard some version of. Stories about his childhood, how he had had no money, how he would walk to school in two feet of snow with holes in his boots, and if he was lucky, he would get one sugar cube to lick—half on the way to school, and half saved so that he had a treat for the walk home. Every time we walked in the door with a bag of candy, the stories would start up again.

My dad was like a chameleon. He could go anywhere and deal with anyone. Our house was always full of people. Some of them would be very successful and some would be very poor. It didn't matter where they came from; to my dad, they were all equal. My siblings and I all inherited that characteristic from him. I quickly discovered I had the gift of getting along with everyone at school. I was able to hang around with the jocks, the academics (who sometimes let me cheat off of them), the yuppies, and the heavy-metal rockers. I could hang with kids who smoked, or who spoke different languages, or who played sports. All of those different people, and I was friends with them all.

Because he could get along with so many different groups, Dad would take us with him to spots that were different than the places most other fathers took their kids—places that were off the beaten track or that weren't considered proper for children. Sadly, there was a lot of poverty in the neighbourhoods where my dad owned his shops. The worst of those neighbourhoods surrounded the Laundromat he owned in Detroit. We would drive over to East Detroit to check in on it, and we would pass through rough neighbourhoods along the way. As we made our way into the building, all of the locals standing outside would greet my dad by name on his way in. "Hi, Johnny," they'd say. We never stayed long—just enough time to check up on the place and pick up the money from the machines. It was my job to take the brown money bag full of coins and cash and put it inside an empty soapbox the size of my chest, and then carry the whole thing to the car. Before we'd leave the building, my dad would say, "Don't make it look like there's money in there." I could barely lift the thing—any other kid would have fallen over trying to lift it up—but I didn't want to let my dad down. I guess that carrying open cartons of money in East Detroit in the 1970s helped me become fearless.

My dad trusted most people, and he went out of his way to help everyone he could. But he eventually got burned trusting so many others. My dad couldn't always cross the border to check on his Laundromat in Detroit, so he hired an employee to help him watch over the business when he wasn't there. It turns out my dad trusted the wrong guy. In one of the periods when my dad didn't drive down to check in, this employee stole all of the cash that the Laundromat made each day. Not only that, but he even had all the washers and dryers cleared out and sold the day before my Dad got back. Then he disappeared; my dad never saw the guy again.

My dad blamed himself, saying it was his fault. That's what he was like—always refusing to talk badly about anyone or blame others. He helped people find houses, get jobs, buy restaurants, and when he went through some tough times, he never showed it. He stayed upbeat and positive. That was the thing that always stuck with me—my dad always made sure to downplay how hard things were when he was going through those rough times. He made it sound like there was always a way to get through whatever struggle he faced. It drove Mom crazy sometimes, but Dad never worried about anything.

Or at least that's the feeling we got around him. If he was ever stressed about anything, he never let on and nobody ever knew about it. I know he must have been stressed at that time, too, because after we lost the one Laundromat, my family went through some down times. We had to sell our family home and move into a small unit at the back of the variety store that my dad owned in Belle River. But because of the example my parents set, none of us let that get us down, and we made a new home. My dad built my grandmother a new greenhouse; I would still buzz around town on my bike—a Yamaha YZ80—with no helmet on; and when my friends came over for sleepovers, we'd camp out in the back of the convenience store and have the run of the place.

There is no question that I was a bit of a wild child when I was young, especially when I wasn't playing sports. Because of that, my brother worked hard to try and keep me in line. I could easily have been a loose cannon, but Dash was tough on me because he wanted people to be proud of me and our family. He kept me on track. There were plenty of other parents who thought I was a bad kid, and they didn't want their kids to hang around me. If only those parents could have seen what their own children were up to. I wasn't a bad kid, but still, sometimes I lived up to my reputation. When I was twelve years old, I decided to knock out my two front teeth so I would look more like Philadelphia Flyers star Bobby Clarke. Now, my dad never hit me, and in general he was a calm guy, but that was the one time he really lost it. He was livid. I didn't realize what the big deal was at the time; I thought that if I knocked out my teeth, more would grow back. But those were my real, adult teeth that I'd broken on the thick chrome handlebars of my bike. Still, I didn't care; all that mattered to me was that I was able to look like Bobby Clarke. Goes to show you what idols can do to you as a kid.

SHIFT WORK

There was no question that Mom was the real disciplinarian in the family. Dad was always hard on Dash because he was the oldest child, but when it came to Trish and me, he was soft. But not Mom, not ever. We all loved each other, but Mom was a strict, old-fashioned woman, and she wouldn't let us get away with anything. When she was frustrated with me, she'd give me a light smack with the broom handle, the flyswatter, shoes, hockey sticks, those plastic race-car tracks—whatever she could get her hands on. We never thought anything of it—it wasn't harmful, and it wasn't a big deal for us to be disciplined. In fact, I made a game out of it. My mom would go to smack me and I would shout, "Palmateer! Palmateer!" and lift my arms up to block her shots. Mike Palmateer was the star goalie for the Leafs back then, so I pretended I was him, blocking shots from my mom. My poor mom couldn't pronounce "Palmateer," and unfortunately, she would end up hurting herself more than she would me. My mom gave up on chasing me around like that when I was thirteen. She'd grabbed a hockey stick, but as soon as she got close to me, I caught the blade of the stick and, with her holding on to the other end, used it to lift her off her feet. After that, she knew there was nothing she could do anymore; my poor mom.

At times while we were growing up, our mom was both a mother and a father to all of us. She was very strong, and she would do whatever she had to do for her kids. That's all that mattered to her. Since my parents were busy all the time, they weren't always able to drive me to my sports games. My whole life revolved around coming home, dropping off one sports bag, grabbing a bite to eat, and then picking up another bag and heading out the door to the next sport I was playing. Mom didn't drive, so we were lucky to live in a town as small as Belle River. There was one taxi in town at the time, and during my first year of hockey, if my dad or one of my aunts or uncles couldn't drive me, my mom would flag the cab down to get me to my practice or game on time. We couldn't afford for me to be taking taxis to my sports all the time, but my mom was determined to get me where I needed to be. I didn't miss a single sporting event growing up. My mom always found a way to make sure I got there. She was amazing in so many ways.

Although I sometimes gave them a hard time, my parents raised me better than I could have ever asked for. I tried to carry myself in a way that showed that, so I was the kind of kid who treated all of my teachers at school with respect. But I had a real problem: I couldn't keep my attention on anything long enough to finish it. So, in every class I was ever in, I was constantly asking the teacher to let me go to the washroom. I remember telling one teacher, Mr. Brachen, that I had a bladder problem as a way of explaining why I had to go to the bathroom so often. I would end up out of the classroom for twenty or thirty minutes; sometimes I wouldn't even come back. I would just wander the halls, talking to everybody, and that way my dyslexia and attention deficit disorder wouldn't affect the rest of the class.

I found out later that the teachers knew what I was doing the whole time. But they also knew that I wasn't using my time to cause trouble. Most of the time, I would just walk to the gym and play sports to keep myself busy. Sports was my medicine; it was how I got by. Of course, the result was that I barely passed most of my classes. My teachers tried to help me, but they couldn't really identify what was wrong with me; we just didn't know then what we know now. I wonder what my fifth-grade teacher, who failed me, would have done if she'd known I was dyslexic. I never disrespected my teachers, though. Most of the time, it was up to me to find a way to get through. A teacher once told my mom that I needed to go to a school for children with learning disabilities. My mom didn't quite understand what that meant, so she replied, "My kid is not stupid!" But my teacher explained the situation more, and my mom realized that this new school might be helpful for me, so we decided to give it a try. After just two weeks, the teachers at the new school contacted my parents to say that I didn't belong there—I was getting perfect scores on their tests, and they didn't feel that I needed the level of help that they provided.

Despite that, I still struggled in school. It was hard to describe what my dyslexia and my short attention span were like as a kid. I would try to tell my dad that I couldn't actually read a book. He wouldn't accept that. He would just say, "You've got to study, you've got to do your homework." I'd try, but I would still confuse my letters; I had no control over how all the c's and s's got mixed up, for example. To me, that's just the way it was. Some of my teachers really helped me get through public school. My eighth-grade teacher, Mr. Parr, and the vice principal, Mr. Glidden, were probably the most help. They were both sports guys and coaches, so they understood me. The other thing that saved me in school was my memory. Since I had a hard time reading books, I learned to read people. I trained myself to pick up on the smallest cues—a person's body language, their tone of voice, the way they approached me—to make up for my lack of reading. And most important, if someone said something or physically demonstrated it to me, I would never forget it. But if I had to read something in a textbook, I was toast.

While I was respectful of all of my teachers, my attention deficit disorder meant that I was often being called out by the impatient ones. Once, in fourth grade, I went so far that the teacher decided to give me the strap. I didn't fight it; I got in trouble enough to know when to push back and when I was better off just accepting what was coming. I got up and stood in front of the teacher, and as he was hitting me with this thick, leather strap, I stared straight at him as if nothing was happening. I didn't say a word, but I gave him that "Are you done?" look. He kept hitting me with the strap, but I gave no reaction, and his frustration started to show. It got to the point that he stood up on a chair and jumped off of it to hit me. It was almost like he was throwing all of his weight into each blow, and he was breaking out into a sweat in the process. As he jumped, I started laughing at him—he couldn't hurt me. When he finally finished and we went outside for recess, the whole class looked at me in silence as I walked out and played soccer. I just acted like nothing had happened. It was at that point that I realized I could take whatever anyone threw at me.

I really don't know why I was so much stronger than the other kids. My family used to joke that it was because I ate so much spinach. My mom's spinach was my favourite meal. She would make spinach pita, and this being the time when Popeye was Popeye, I was one of those kids who believed that the more spinach you ate, the stronger you got. But I wasn't just the strongest kid in our area growing up; I was also the mentally toughest. Looking back, I realize that our childhood helped make me that way. I come from humble beginnings. Everything I have in life, I have earned. Nobody gave me anything, nor did I expect anything from them. If I wanted something, I had to earn it. It was that way when I was young, and it is still that way today.

While my academics were an issue, sports never were. As a kid, I would often play sports with Dash and his friends. Dash is almost five years older than me, which meant that I was playing against kids his age. That could have been a setback, but I soon figured out that I wasn't just keeping up with Dash and his older friends at sports; I was actually beating them. At fourteen, I was even taking on adults in arm-wrestling competitions and winning those. Dash can vouch for me—I have never lost an arm-wrestling match, now or then.

By the time I entered high school, I was confident that there was no one around me that I should be afraid of. When I started ninth grade, I was given locker number 212, and I never put a lock on it. I didn't need one. I knew that if someone messed with my stuff, I could deal with them. But I also knew that nobody ever would.

As a kid, hockey wasn't my best sport. In fact, I didn't even start playing hockey until I was nine years old. I had no business getting on the ice that year—I couldn't even skate! My dad had to sponsor our jerseys just so I would be given a spot on the team. I spent the first few games skating on my ankles, and at my first practice, I didn't let go of the boards once. But over the course of the season, I learned the basic skills. I was determined and worked hard to get better, and by the end of the year, we had won the league championship and I'd been named the MVP. It was at that moment that my dream of being a pro hockey player was born.

Despite my hockey dreams, soccer was easily my number-one sport as a kid. I still think one of the reasons I made it as a hockey player is that I was always a good all-around athlete. As a kid, a junior, and a pro, I wasn't just a hockey player. Playing other sports—and believe me, I played every sport I could—made me a better hockey player. Playing so much soccer when I was young really helped build up my legs, and that went a long way towards making me a better skater.

At sixteen, I actually almost moved away from hockey forever. That year, I received an offer to go play soccer professionally for a team in Europe. Not long after that, other offers from overseas started to come in, and I found myself with an opportunity to move to half a dozen countries across the pond. But my father turned them all down; he didn't like the idea of me moving to Europe alone as a teenager. It didn't matter how much money I was offered—it was never an option.

So I stayed in Belle River, and I started to distinguish myself in a few different sports: soccer, basketball, baseball, volleyball, and football. By the time I started high school, I had won a championship in every one. A couple of years before I started high school, my baseball team won the peewee all-Ontario championship. After we won, the mayor of Belle River was there to help us celebrate, and he started placing the championship medals over everybody's head like it was the Olympics. As he was coming towards me, I thought, That thing isn't fitting over my head. Sure enough, the mayor gets to me and the ribbon of the medal gets stuck on the top of my head. It didn't faze me. Rather than have the mayor try to force the thing, I just grabbed the medal and walked off the stage with the whole town watching. What can I say? My head was my head, and it's been big my whole life.

When I was in ninth grade, we won the regional football championship. This would have been in November 1984, when I was playing for the Belle River Nobles. In our final game that season, I accounted for 12 points, including a 43-yard field goal, as we beat the Amherst Generals 18–14 to capture the ECSSA junior football title. The game was held at the University of Windsor, and I played middle linebacker, kicker, and fullback; I didn't leave the field. Some US college scouts had come down that weekend to watch our senior team play, but most of them ended up watching me kick instead. It didn't faze me, though. I knew college football would never be an option for me because of my academics.

For a time, I was a big fish in a small pond in Belle River. In the same way that my dad successfully owned and operated so many different businesses, I was successfully competing in whatever sport I tried. And it had given me a taste for winning. I was becoming a better athlete by the day, and I wanted more. More challenges, more opportunities, and more championships. But to make that happen, I had some tough decisions to make.

2

Junior Days

W HEN I was twelve years old, there was a tough kid in our neighbourhood who was harassing my older brother, Dash. This kid—well, *kid* might be the wrong word, as I was five years younger than this guy at the time—made it known that he wanted to fight Dash, but my brother always just laughed it off. One day, Dash and I were walking through our neighbourhood when this guy came up and started pushing Dash around again. I had had enough. I was tired of seeing this bully get on Dash's case. Dash was my big brother. I looked up to him, and I would have done anything to protect him. This guy was on top of my brother, punching him, so I jumped into the mix, pushed him off Dash, and lost it. He didn't know what hit him. The kid had hair that was so blond it was almost white, but by the time our fight was done, it was covered in blood.

Dash and I made our way home after our fight, but a little while later, we were surprised by the doorbell. We could hear a voice talking to my mom as she answered the front door. Dash got to my mom first, and I heard a man say, "Look what your son did to my son." I walked up, and I saw the dad pointing to his son's head, which was covered in blood. So I stuck my head in and said, "I'm sorry, sir, but he was beating up my brother."

The father paused and looked at his kid. "*He* beat you up?" he asked his son, pointing down at me. The dad turned around and kicked his son in the butt, yelling at him to get home. He couldn't believe that a little twelve-year-old kid had beaten up a seventeen-year-old.

Trish, Dash, and I didn't have a cushy suburban childhood. But life on the street turned out to be a good training ground for surviving my later life as a hockey player. When I was growing up in Belle River, our family spent the summers in a tough neighbourhood in the west end of Toronto known as the Junction. Back in the early 1970s, the Junction wasn't a bad area. But by the time we started spending the summers there in the late 1970s and early '80s, things had changed. The neighbourhood was full of industrial lands, and at times you could smell the factory fumes when you were out on the street. But the Toronto Albanian community that my parents visited was located mostly in the Junction, so of course that was where we spent most of our time. I ended up doing a lot of street fighting during that period. You didn't have to go far to find someone who was willing to fight back then. I would go out with friends or Dash, and they'd get me into bars—like Misty's, up at the airport—so that they could enter me in arm-wrestling contests to win cash or drinks. I never lost. And when you had guys drinking and getting smoked in an arm-wrestling competition by a kid my age and size, it usually meant that, by the end of the night, I would end up in a fight.

Of course, through all this, I was starting to play hockey at higher and higher levels. I had no idea at the time, but I was experiencing things that other kids in the junior leagues never would have, and as a result, I was constantly toughening myself up, both physically and mentally. It served me well on the rink. When I had been playing in bantam as a thirteen-year-old, I had never really fought on the ice. But when I started playing Junior C for the Belle River Canadiens at fourteen, that changed completely. Suddenly, I was fighting, and beating, twenty-year-olds. I didn't feel as though I were a mean kid; I was always just fearless and driven. And even though I was younger and smaller than most of the guys I squared off against, I never backed down. Nobody ever intimidated me. I just couldn't—and didn't—let myself think that way. My dad used to tell us that he saw death many times during his days in Albania. Everything else after that was nothing to him. My dad truly feared nothing in his life, not even his own death. If he had never shown any fear after all the things he went through in his life, what did I have to be scared about?

It was during my time playing Junior C for Belle River that I first met Ted Lindsay, the Detroit Red Wings legend. Our coach that year—the 1984–85 season—was Marcel Pronovost, Lindsay's former teammate with the Red Wings. I will never forget the day that Pronovost first came to our house. It was just before my parents were about to move to Toronto. At the time, I had already started with the Belle River Canadiens, but I was also still playing basketball, soccer, and football at school. Pronovost, or "Mr. Marcel" as my mom used to call him, very respectfully but very directly said, "Mrs. Domi, Tie can't play four sports at the same time anymore. He has to pick one."

That wasn't hard to do, mostly because I didn't have a choice. After hearing Pronovost out, my mom just said to me, "My boy, you're only playing hockey, because Mr. Marcel said so."

Little did I know, that changed my life forever. Marcel was a hockey legend. An NHL All-Star and a Stanley Cup champion who played over 1,200 games in the NHL, Pronovost had earned a reputation as a physical player who rarely missed time because of injuries. I admired his toughness on the ice and his appreciation for the game. And my mom really respected Pronovost because he was an older gentleman and was always so polite and classy. So when she agreed that I was only going to play hockey, the decision was final. My dad never really cared about hockey until I started playing major junior a few years later. In the early stages, my mom and Dash were far more active when it came to my hockey career.

In that 1984–85 season, we ended up beating Midland in five games to win the Ontario Hockey Association all-Ontario championship, and Pronovost had Ted Lindsay come and speak at our championship banquet in the spring. Lindsay had a lot of great advice that night, but one line sticks with me. In his speech, he said, "It doesn't matter where you're from or how big you are. If you have the heart and the mental toughness, you can do anything."

Those words really meant something to me. As a young, small guy, hearing "Terrible Ted" Lindsay tell us we could overcome anything was a huge inspiration. Lindsay had won Stanley Cups, he'd battled hockey executives to make the league better for players, and he'd been such a fierce competitor that the league literally had to create penalties because of the way he played. But he still took the time to stop and talk with us, a Junior C hockey team from Belle River, and make us feel important. Years later, when I was forty-two years old, I went to a legendary restaurant in Detroit called Joe Muer's and I met the owner, Joe, for the first time. He told me that I reminded him of Ted Lindsay. As soon as I heard that, my mind went back to the lessons that Lindsay had passed to my team in Junior C. A big reason I was even sitting in that steak house was Marcel Pronovost and Ted Lindsay and the impact they had on my hockey career. Both of them had been great players and great men, so I told Joe what a pleasure it was to meet him, and what an honour it was to even be mentioned in the same sentence as icons like Lindsay and Pronovost.

* * *

After that winning season with the Canadiens, I moved up to play Junior B for the Windsor Bulldogs. Through forty-two games in the 1985–86 season, I scored eight goals and racked up 346 penalty minutes. I learned early on in that season that I was always going to have to be ready to react and do whatever job I was given. Usually, that meant that I had to be ready to fight guys a lot bigger than me who wanted to knock my head off. That was my job, and I felt a responsibility to take care of my teammates. A lot of people doubted I would be able to sustain the kind of intensity and toughness I showed when I entered junior, and over time, as I proved them wrong, those same doubters became jealous of my popularity and my success.

For all of the fights I have had in my life, both on and off the ice, I have only been in the back of a cop car once. It happened during my Junior B season after one of our games against Tillsonburg.

I beat up a chicken. A six-foot, six-inch Tillsonburg chicken *mascot*, to be precise.

This mascot stood behind the penalty box through most of the game. So every time I went in the penalty box (which happened pretty often), he was right behind me. He was huge and dressed like a real chicken, and he spent the whole time flapping his arms and mocking my big head. The stuff this guy said really got on my nerves, so while I was in the box, I yelled over the glass, "I'll see you after the game." As soon as the game finished, I took off my skates, threw on my running shoes, and a bunch of my teammates followed me out of the dressing room. I found the chicken waiting for me in the concourse, and we started throwing punches right away. He had no chance.

Next thing I knew, I was sitting in the back of a police car. Of course, the cops had to take in the mascot, too. But while I was quietly and comfortably sitting in the back of the cop car, this guy was so big in his costume that the cops had to cram him into the front seat, chicken head and all. Turns out the guy was a lot older than me. The cops asked the mascot, "Did you know he was underage?" I was only fifteen at the time. The guy in the suit was shocked, and more than a little embarrassed, that he'd been beaten up by an underage kid. When the cops finally let both of us go, I got on the team bus with all of my equipment still on—I'd kept my teammates waiting long enough. Everybody got a good laugh out of it on the way home.

That was the key. I wasn't just the strongest kid on the team; I was also the mentally toughest. No matter what happened, I had to be able to laugh things off, move on, and focus on the next challenge. I was far from the best player in the league, or even on my own team. But my fearlessness and toughness, especially my mental strength and my ability to withstand so much pain and injury, set me apart. It was enough to even draw the attention of some Ontario Hockey League scouts, and at the end of the season, there was a good chance that I would be drafted in the OHL Priority Selection—basically the major junior draft. The OHL was just one step below the pro leagues, and it was (and still is) known as the best platform for guys who dreamed of making the NHL. Although I'd caught some scouts' eyes, I still wasn't exactly a top prospect coming out of Junior B. At the OHL draft that June, round after round went by without my name being called. Eventually, I figured that the attention I'd been getting was just temporary. I was disappointed, and I assumed that my dream wasn't going to happen, so I gathered my things and started to head out before the draft was even finished. But then, just as I was leaving the building, I heard my name called. I had been selected 102nd overall, by the Peterborough Petes. I couldn't believe my luck. In two years, I'd gone from playing Junior C in Belle River to the staging ground for the NHL: the Ontario Hockey League.

I was still just a kid, only sixteen years old, when my first year in the OHL began. The season really kicked into gear, though, on September 26, 1986, when we were set to play the Kingston Canadians. Not only was Kingston a good team, but it also had arguably the fiercest guy in the OHL on its roster: Marc Laforge. Laforge was huge at six foot three and 215 pounds, and he was far and away the toughest guy in the league at the time.

Before that first game, our coach, Dick Todd, came into the dressing room and gave us his pregame talk. As he wrapped up, he said, "And remember, I don't want anybody fighting number 18 out there. Except one guy." All of a sudden, all eyes in the room turned towards me. That was when I realized what I was getting myself into. I should have been freaked out—I was only sixteen— but I wasn't. Crazy as it might sound, I was actually looking forward to the fight.

On my first shift of the game, I lined up across from Laforge, and as we waited for the puck to drop, I looked up at him and asked, "You ready to go?" Laforge thought I was joking; he didn't even look at me. So I said, "Soon as this puck drops, we're going." Sure enough, as soon as the puck hit the ice, I dropped my gloves and forced him to do the same. We backed up towards the corner, and as I went to grab Laforge's jersey, he landed a couple of lefts. But I toughed it out, got a hold of him, and pulled him in, and as we grappled by the faceoff dot, I put my leg behind his and flipped Laforge to the ice where I threw punches down on him. The linesmen broke us up almost immediately after that, so it wasn't much of a fight, but it didn't matter—word got around the league that I'd beaten the toughest guy in the league my first time in an OHL uniform, and I found myself with a new reputation overnight.

Right then, my career changed. All of a sudden, I was expected to fight teams' toughest guys on a regular basis. And so I did. My new status as the guy to beat in the OHL could have worn me out. But everything I had learned and gone through as a kid up until then allowed me to withstand the new challenges I was facing. Dick Todd didn't force me to fight Laforge that first night. In fact, he never told me to fight anyone. Not once in my career did a coach ever tell me directly to go out and fight. If one actually *had* told me to go out there and fight for him, I probably would have turned around and hit him instead. If I had to fight to protect the guys on either side of me, I would do it without a moment's hesitation. My teammates knew I was ready to drop the gloves for them at any moment in any game we played. And if they didn't know, they found out. But I didn't want someone else telling me to fight for the wrong reasons. Every fight was a choice, one that I had to make for the right reasons.

* * *

I had a job to do, a team to protect, and a coach who knew how to push me. But I have to admit, my first year in the OHL wasn't great. In fact, at one point I nearly quit and walked away from hockey altogether. Even though I'd beaten Laforge in my first shift with the Petes and earned a new status in the league, I didn't play a lot of games during that first year in Peterborough. It wasn't for anything that I'd done with the Petes; it was because of all the fighting I'd done while I was playing with Windsor the year before. In that season with Windsor, I'd had a lot of fights, and everyone in Junior B had to wear helmets with cages. Punching those cages over and over did a lot of damage to my hands. The knuckles on my left hand, in particular, were a mess, and the doctors decided that they would have to operate on me to push the knuckles back to their natural positions. So that summer between my Junior B season and my start with the Petes, I had the surgery. The doctors reset my knuckles and then inserted metal rods to hold them in place for three months. But that wasn't the worst of it. After those three months were up, the doctors had to pull the metal rods back out of my hands. I have a high pain tolerance, but I will never be able to describe the agony I felt that day. With all of the pain and rehab that I had to go through, my hands took a long time to get back to normal, and that meant that in my first year with the Petes, I really didn't get to play much.

On top of all that, I was really homesick. I missed my friends and family, especially my mom and dad. So one day, I wrote a note on the chalkboard in the dressing room: "Good luck guys, nice to meet you all. Tie."

Because I had had to move away from home to play with the Petes, the team had arranged for me to live with a family from Peterborough—a typical setup for junior hockey players. Mr. Ellis, my billet that first year, and Kevin McDonald, an overage player who was my roommate, were the ones who drove me to the bus station. On the way, they tried to talk me out of leaving, asking me if I was sure I wanted to go through with it. When we got to the bus station, my mind was made up, so I thanked the two of them and walked away. I was all set to take a Greyhound bus back home to Toronto and give up my hockey career right there and then.

But as soon as I stepped onto the bus, I stopped. Something shifted inside me, and suddenly I couldn't let myself just walk away. Sure, I could have given up because things were hard and weren't going the way I wanted. But that wasn't how I was raised, and that wasn't how I wanted my time in hockey to end. Even though I was homesick, I was not a quitter. And if I had left, I would have been known as a quitter. And there is no way I ever wanted to be thought of that way. So I got off the bus, got back in the car, and went right back to where I'd left off.

That first year in Peterborough was tough for me to understand. Up until then, sports had come so easily to me. But being a rookie in the OHL can be hard. And being a rookie in the OHL when you aren't the most skilled player is even tougher. I had to do what I'd always done, what my dad had taught me all those years: I had to work harder.

It wasn't easy, but I managed to find my way through that first year. And after the season was over, I moved back to Toronto and got a summer job at the Ontario Food Terminal. As difficult as that year with the Petes was, the time I spent at the Food Terminal that summer was way rougher. I knew that athletes work hard. But I doubt any athlete my age worked as hard as I did that summer. The guys at the Food Terminal worked non-stop without questions or excuses, from dawn to dusk every single day. Working out and practising is nothing compared to spending your entire day slugging crates of food. Every day that summer, I started work at 6 a.m. and didn't stop until after 5 p.m. Each day was the same as the one before. The trucks would roll in and I would help unload crates of food, stacking and unstacking these giant watermelons all day long. I got a feel for what it means to really work for a living, and I just knew it wasn't what I wanted to do for the rest of my life. I gained a whole new view of training and practising, too. If I could spend all day unloading watermelons and crates of food, then I sure as hell could push myself and train harder to become a better hockey player. So every day that I was slugging those boxes, I would say to myself, "I want to be a hockey player." I kept telling myself that I just had to make it, no matter what.

In my second year with the Petes, we had eleven rookies on our team. One of those rookies was a talented kid and a highly touted prospect by the name of Mike Ricci. In Ricci's last year before joining the Petes, he'd scored 39 goals and 81 points in only 38 games. One day, early into the season, Ricci came into the dressing room and Dick Todd looked at me and said, "Tie, you're going to play with Mike Ricci." And that was that. It wasn't a major, scripted moment. But it was a surprising move. I had no clue it was going to happen. I mean, I was coming off a season where I had played only eighteen games, with a grand total of one goal and one assist.

Honestly, I didn't think I was a good hockey player until I started playing on the same line as Ricci. I earned more playing time as my second year went on, and my confidence just grew and grew. And in anything you do, the more confidence you have, the better you become. Soon we were the team's top line. Facing off against other teams' skilled players, I began to notice that nobody was hitting me. I realized that, thanks to the fights I'd won as a rookie, word had gone around the league to leave me alone. All of a sudden, I was getting room on the ice, and I started to think to myself that I might score a few goals. Even better, I figured out how to feed Ricci and the other guys the puck. With me on the ice, nobody was hitting Ricci, and he made the extra space count, which meant that I ended up with a lot of assists that year.

There's no question that I only earned that opportunity to play with Ricci by fighting all the way through Junior B, Junior C, and my first year in the OHL. My skills developed that year, but only because my toughness had come first. That's what let me carve out the extra time and space that I needed to become a well-rounded hockey player. I was seventeen, and for the first time, my hard work was creating a really major opportunity for me. I skated hard every shift and pushed myself every practice to make sure that I wouldn't waste the opportunity I'd earned. It's one thing to get your foot in the door. It's another to keep it there.

My personal life was even better that second year, too. Ricci's father and my dad got along great. My sister, Trish, said it was hilarious to see the two of them sitting beside each other in the stands, watching us play. Like two peas in a pod, she described it. They were these two short European immigrants, and since my dad spoke some Italian, the two of them would sit there and talk in Italian the whole time. My mom was never there—she only came to one game in my junior career. Trish told me she just couldn't handle it—she was too scared that I would get hurt.

My dad had a lighter approach. He called the penalty box "jail." Whenever he saw me head to the penalty box, he'd say to the rest of the family, "There he is, in jail again. That's good. He can stay there in jail."

At the start of the 1987–88 season, I said to Dick Todd, "We're going to the finals." When I said that, I don't think Dick really thought it was possible, especially since the team was made up mostly of rookies. But as the year went on, my prediction looked more and more like it would come true. Everything clicked for us that year in Peterborough, and despite our lack of experience, we ended up finishing at the top of our division. The next thing you know, we had not only made it all the way to the OHL finals, but we'd swept both of our first two series to get there.

I can still remember getting on the bus on the way to the opening game of the OHL finals. I said to Dick, "I told you we would make it to the finals." He didn't miss a beat. He turned back to me and said, "Hey, kid, now we got to win it."

We were set to play against Adam Graves and a stacked Windsor Spitfires team. We had won 44 games that year and had 93 points, but Graves and the Spitfires ended up winning 50 games and led the entire league with 102 points. And just like us Petes, the Spitfires were also a perfect 8-0 in the opening rounds of the playoffs.

Well, we didn't get it done that year. Graves and the Spitfires beat us in four straight games. They were the better team, and it really showed. But even though we didn't win it all that season, I am proud to say that Dick Todd was named the OHL's coach of the year. We had started off the season as a team full of rookies that no one gave a chance, and we had come together to form a team that could compete with the best of the league at the time.

And personally, playing on that line with Mike Ricci, I ended up scoring 22 goals with 292 PIMs (penalties in minutes) during the regular season, with another 12 points in the playoffs. I had come a long way from my first year in the OHL.

Even though we fell short in 1988, we were already looking ahead to the next season. Everything was starting to click, and the timing couldn't have been better, because in 1988–89 there would be some important people around the NHL taking notice of what was happening with me and the Petes.

3

Entering the Show

As I made my way through junior hockey, I certainly had a dream—to play in the NHL—and I was doing everything I could to stay on the right track and make it happen. Towards the end of my second year with the Petes, I started to believe my dream might actually come true. Late in that 1987–88 season, when we made a run to the OHL finals, scouts started showing up to some of our key games. We tried not to pay too much attention to them, focusing instead on the games in front of us. But it was easy to get distracted when you saw Leafs legends like Johnny Bower, George Armstrong, and Dick Duff in the stands.

Those guys were always a three-pack, my three favourite old-timers for the Maple Leafs. I never got to see them play, but I knew their history, and they were guys I respected—not only for their achievements, but because of the way they could still joke with each other and play around years after they'd finished playing together on the Leafs. It was cool to see. These three guys were also the men who were scouting me, and as they showed up to more and more games, I started to realize that the Leafs were interested in me. So I started to work even harder to make the best impression I could, and I managed to impress them in a few key games.

The high point of my season came in one of our games at Maple Leaf Gardens against the Toronto Marlboros. The Leafs' owner, Harold Ballard, was even at the game in his bunker. On my way to scoring a hat trick that night, I also had one of my best fights of my junior career against a guy named Glenn Lowes. I think that game went a long way towards showing the scouts that I wasn't just a fighter, that I could play and hold my own against anyone else in the league.

I didn't hear from the Leafs during the rest of that season with the Petes as we made our way to the finals, but in June 1988, I found myself at the Forum in Montreal for the NHL entry draft. I remember driving to Montreal for the draft with my agent at the time. My agent was also representing Rob Ray, a guy I chased around in junior and fought a few times, and we picked him up in a farm town halfway between Toronto and Montreal. He and I were playfully wrestling in the car on the way to the draft. It was just the way we were.

I remember when Rob got drafted in the fifth round. I was so excited for him. Rob was even more excited—I remember watching him climb a telephone pole on St. Catherine Street and laughing my head off as he swung from the top of it. I'd never seen anything like it. Rob and I were roommates at the draft, but we didn't become longtime friends after that. Rob started in the league at the same time I did, and he ended up being one of my biggest rivals for the longest period of my career. He and I were there in the old-school era when teams' tough guys would drop the gloves and get it over with on the first shift, just to set the tone. We both had a job to do, and we respected each other for it. It turns out our careers would mirror each other as we each made the transition from fighter to player to change with the times.

In the second round, twenty-seventh overall, I heard my name announced by Gord Stellick, the Toronto Maple Leafs' general manager at the time. I was in a total daze, but I managed to stand up, hug my dad and Dash, and make my way down to shake Gord's hand. As I stood in front of the NHL logo in my new Leafs jersey for my official draft photo, I couldn't believe how far my journey had already taken me. It had only been two years since I stood on the steps of that Greyhound bus, thinking my hockey career was over. Now I had taken an important step closer to a pro career.

* * *

In the fall of 1988, I went back to Peterborough for a final season with the Petes. That last season in junior was a blur. Between attending Leafs training camp at the beginning of the season and sustaining a broken ankle a little while later, I ended up only playing 43 out of 66 regular season games that year. Still, I was so excited that I was going to have a chance to realize my dream of becoming a pro hockey player. And it seemed like I would enter that next chapter on the right foot, because despite missing nearly a third of the season, my last year in junior was also my most successful.

Although we'd fallen short in the OHL finals the previous year, we were back in the championship series again in the spring of 1989, this time against the Niagara Falls Thunder. For the first four games of the series, we traded wins back and forth. Our third game was a blowout—we beat the Thunder 11–3, and I even managed to score a hat trick. Everything seemed to be going our way that game. We were scoring in bunches and silencing the crowd minute by minute. We were confident and believed in each other. Then, with five minutes left, the Niagara crowd decided to show their unhappiness. The arena was packed that game, and they'd been on me all night long. The fans had a stuffed monkey that they had dressed up in a Peterborough Petes jersey. And of course, it was my name and number on the back of that jersey. They would take the monkey—which had a banana in its mouth—wrap a rope around its neck, and hang it over the glass above the ice. The monkey didn't faze me; I actually thought it was pretty funny. In the dying minutes of that game, one fan walked up to the edge of the boards and flung a banana on the ice. My teammates didn't know whether to laugh or be embarrassed for me. I looked at the fan and then at the stuffed monkey hanging over the glass. I skated over to the banana, peeled it next to the referee, took a bite, and then tossed the peel back into the stands. Nobody could believe I'd done it. The whole building shut up.

But Niagara came right back to take game four before we managed to get ahead in the series by winning the fifth game. That brought us to Niagara Falls on May 1 for what turned out to be the final game of our series against the Thunder. And believe me, that was a crazy night—the stands were packed before the warm-up even ended.

The game started off on an intense note. As I skated laps during the warm-up, I saw that the door to the Niagara bench was open. That was unusual, so I looked over and was surprised to see Niagara's coach, Bill LaForge, standing there. He looked at me, and as I passed close to the Thunder's bench, he started screaming at me.

"They're coming, Domi! My tough guys are coming. You better be ready, Domi!"

I knew LaForge was trying to get in my head, but he couldn't faze me. I couldn't get rattled then, and I can't get rattled now. But LaForge kept chirping me as I warmed up, and it was starting to get on my nerves. So on one lap, I grabbed a puck from centre ice and sent a wrist shot right at his shins. He howled as it stung him dead on. He kept the bench door closed after that.

In my first shift of the game, I decided that, rather than let Niagara get any momentum, I had to set the tone of the game right away. LaForge had said I should watch out for guys coming after me, but rather than wait for that, I decided to take the fight to them. As we lined up for a faceoff, I looked over to the Niagara bench and yelled, "Who's first?"

Nobody could match my stare. This was a tough, skilled team with guys like Dennis Vial, Brad May, Scott Pearson, and Keith Primeau, and I was waiting to see who would look at me, but I didn't catch one eyeball. I knew that we weren't going to have any issues that night, and all of my teammates got the room they needed to play. Sure enough, at the end of the game, our entire team was on the ice, celebrating. We were the OHL champions. We'd finished what we'd started a couple of years earlier and gone from a bunch of rookies playing together for the first time to provincial junior champions in just two years.

* * *

Winning the OHL title was easily the highlight of my junior career. And after the season, I felt I had nothing left to prove in the junior ranks. I felt more than ready for the pro game. But as you can imagine, there is a world of difference between playing in the NHL and playing in junior. I knew from my first experience at the Leafs' training camp the year before that there was more work to be done before I would truly be ready, and I knew it was up to me to figure out what I needed to do. For most of the 1989–90 season, I played with the Leafs' American Hockey League farm team, the Newmarket Saints, developing my skills and learning the way the pro game worked. I learned to pick out who was a good team player and who was in it for himself. When you protect your teammates, your job is a lot easier if you know that the guys around you appreciate your job.

Towards the end of my season in Newmarket, I finally got my chance to make my NHL debut with the Leafs. It was March 2, 1990, and we were playing the Red Wings in Detroit that night. This was my chance to make my mark, and I wanted to make it count. I didn't waste any time: on my first shift, I dropped my gloves and started trading punches with Kevin McClelland. The refs broke up the fight almost right after it started, and on top of the fighting penalty, I ended up getting a misconduct to boot. It was my first NHL game, and I ended up with 37 penalty minutes.

Between periods in the dressing room, I found it hilarious when I discovered Al Iafrate and Chris Kotsopoulos in the two bathroom stalls. They were both sitting on the toilet with their full hockey gear on, having a cigarette. This was an open dressing room, and there was smoke everywhere. I thought to myself, Well, this is the NHL. That's just the way things were back then. It was everything I'd been working towards for years, and I expected the atmosphere and the game to all feel new or different in some way. But after one more game with the Leafs, I was sent right back to Newmarket. I spent the rest of the year down in the minors, but I didn't mind.

I'd had a taste of the big show, and I knew that I would work my way back.

My reintroduction to the big leagues didn't happen in a Leafs sweater, though. After just one year with the Leafs organization, I was traded to the New York Rangers. It was June 28, 1990, and I was on the golf course when I was directed into the pro shop to take a call. When I got the message that it was the Leafs' general manager at the time, Floyd Smith, on the phone for me, I thought it was a joke. What could be so urgent that he'd call me on the golf course? When I picked up the phone, I found out: I had been traded to the New York Rangers. And that was that. I didn't know what was happening. I was just starting to get a feel for pro hockey as part of the Leafs organization, and then suddenly, one phone call later, I was a Ranger. I didn't know how to feel or what to think about it; it was all just so sudden. What I didn't realize then, but would come to learn, was that hockey is a business. What I also had no way of knowing that day in June was that getting dealt to New York would turn out to be very good for both my career and my personal life.

I spent most of the rest of the summer getting ready to move to New York. My brother, Dash, was a hairdresser at the time, and he gave me a haircut before I took off for my first training camp with the Rangers. I was driving a Honda Accord, and I was about to get into the car when Dash called me back. I could tell he was getting choked up with me, his kid brother, getting ready to take off for New York. I will never forget what he told me: "Do *not* give them a reason to send you home."

Believe me, I was prepared to do anything to make it.

I gave it everything I had in that training camp. After a year of playing in the minors, paying attention and working hard, I knew what was expected of me and what I would be up against in camp.

I didn't want to spend another year in the AHL; I wanted a spot on the big-league roster. So I made the best use I could of the experience I'd gained and the lessons I'd learned in Newmarket. But before I got a chance to start with the Rangers, I had a brief stint in Binghamton, New York, with the Rangers' AHL team. The Rangers wanted me to work on my game before they brought me back up. My last game with Binghamton was in Halifax. I had four goals and an assist by the end of the second period, but I didn't get to play the third. Our captain, Peter Laviolette, was being beaten up by Kevin Kaminski. To protect my captain, I jumped into the fight. Unfortunately, being the third man into a fight earned me an immediate game misconduct, which meant an automatic ejection from the game.

I went out that night with the rest of the team, and I was buying drinks for everyone. I was buying drinks for the other team, too, even Greg Smyth, who was Halifax's tough guy and whom I'd fought a few times before. The next morning at practice, I was half-dressed for practice when John Paddock, our coach, called me out into the hallway.

"What time did you get in last night?" he asked.

I stalled. I didn't want John thinking I'd been out all night or up to no good. But before I could say anything, John continued.

"I'm kidding. Take your gear off and pack up. You have to get on a plane. You're playing in Washington tonight for the Rangers."

It took me two different flights to get from Halifax to Washington. I got to the arena so late that I missed the warm-up. When I finally got to the locker room, I opened my bag and found that the veterans from Binghamton had put some beer bottles in my bag. Of course, my bag had been tossed around on those flights, and the bottles had burst. All of my gear was soaked with beer.

The game was about to start, so I had to wear the beer-drenched equipment. I finally got to the bench, and after a couple of minutes, our coach, Roger Neilson, made a face and asked, "For crap's sake, who smells like beer?"

I had known Roger since our time in Peterborough, and he was so straitlaced that I found it hard to even swear around him. I called Roger over and explained the situation, and he laughed it off. Then, suddenly, I was over the boards for my first shift.

John Kordic, whom I called "Chippy" when I played with him on the Leafs because of his big cheeks, was with the Capitals at the time. John was a fun-loving guy. When I got on the ice, the first thing he said to me was, "Let's go, Tie." I didn't want to fight Chippy, so I tried to laugh it off, but he insisted that we fight. So we dropped the gloves. It was a fight I didn't want to have, but I did get the better of him. John was pretty pissed about it, so he was yelling at me in the hallway afterward.

"I told you that you didn't want to do it," I reminded him. Luckily, things cooled down after that and we moved on.

During training camp, I tried to get familiar with my new teammates and my new town. At one point, Bernie Nicholls, our top centremen, lent me his Jaguar convertible. Nicholls was one of our star players, and in those days, high-end guys like him would take care of tough guys, just like we'd take care of them. So even though I was only twenty years old, and Bernie and I had barely met, he just tossed me the keys to his Jag and said, "Here, take it." I drove across Forty-Second Street, down Broadway, and through Times Square in that gorgeous Jag, thinking I had already made it. I had no plan, no cares—I was just cruising wherever I wanted with an entire season ahead of me. I felt like a million bucks!

Of course, in reality, I hadn't done shit yet. I was making

$110,000 a year—not bad for a young guy, but still far less than the guys around me. I was making more in endorsements than I was from my base salary. Still, the money didn't really matter at the time; I was young, playing in the NHL, and living in New York City. What could possibly be better?

* * *

I had four roommates during my time with the Rangers: Joe Cirella, Lindy Ruff, Joey Kocur, and Adam Graves. My first roommate was Cirella, a veteran defenceman. I used to call Joe "Mama" because, when we were on the road, he would fold all of my clothes, right down to my dirty underwear. He had everything down pat—through his own version of room service, everything would be organized perfectly in the room and wake-up calls were always set. At times, things were so organized that I thought I was rooming with my mom, and so Joe became "Mama." Later on, I became more of a germophobe and an organization freak myself, and I insisted on folding everything I took with me on the road— Joe clearly made an impression on me! I always wondered what kind of impression I made on him.

My second roommate was Lindy Ruff. Rooming with him, it didn't take long to discover what a great practical joker he is. Fans who see him standing behind a bench now as he coaches a team may not realize this, but Lindy Ruff has a great sense of humour. He's easily one of the funniest guys I played with. All the guys I played with early in my career were fun and taught me the ropes in one way or another. You learn a lot of different things from a lot of people, and you always have to take what you think is best from everyone, because you never know what or who may help you. But at the end of the day, it's your call. Mark Messier taught me everything I know about leadership. Joe Kocur taught me how to be a better fighter. And Lindy Ruff taught me a lot about the art of the practical joke, because he was the master. Practical jokes and having fun are important to a team. There is a ton of stress on hockey players throughout the season, and the more times you can have a good laugh to relieve some of the tension, the calmer and better the team will play.

The best prank that Lindy ever pulled on me happened after one of our practices. Lindy got off the ice right away and hustled back to the dressing room. Another surprising fact about Lindy is that he's very good with a needle and thread. Before I even got off the ice, Lindy had sewn the cuffs of my pants about two inches higher than normal. Not only that, but after I got back to the dressing room and showered, as I went to put my clothes on, I found that my shoes were nailed to the bench. When I'd finally gotten my shoes free, I thought that was the end of the joke, so I didn't notice what Lindy had done to my pants. I got changed, and then I went out into the hallway to sign autographs for the fans. I made my way down the roped-off section of the hallway to the bus, and I couldn't understand why everyone was laughing. Of course, everybody on the team knew what was up. When I got to the bus, I saw all of the guys' heads poking out into the aisle to check out my pants. That was when I finally clued in. I walked past Tony Amonte and Doug Weight, who were laughing so hard they were crying, and I took my pants off. The veterans like to have fun with the rookies. I always took the jokes well, but this time, I think Lindy thought I might kill him. But the prank was just too good not to laugh about it! That moment was my welcome to the NHL.

In each of my first four games with the Rangers, I was in at least one fight. And although I wasn't playing every game, I knew there would be more to come and that I might be called upon any night to step in and protect my teammates. I was playing on the fourth line, usually with Joe Kocur, and he was one of the toughest guys in the league; between the two of us, I would argue that there was no tougher duo in the NHL at the time. Joey had lots of incredible advice for me. He taught me to never waste my punches. Before or after the games, Joey never talked about fighting or the tough assignments he'd faced. I never liked to talk about it either, and Joey assured me that ours was the right approach—it's a hard enough job to do, so don't talk about it. When Joey—whom I called "Papa"—and I were roommates with the Rangers, we used to play cards until four in the morning. We wouldn't drink or party; we would just sit in our hotel room and play cards against each other nonstop. It was our way of finding some quiet and calm after a game, of escaping the physical and mental pressures that came with playing our style of hockey. Those card games were incredibly valuable to me. No matter how tough you are, everyone needs to be able to take their mind off things.

*   *   *

In the second half of the 1990–91 season, I was spending more time with the Rangers in New York and less time in the minor leagues with their AHL affiliate, the Binghamton Rangers. It was an exciting change from my year in the Leafs system, and I was happy to be taking a step in the right direction. My work was getting results, too, and on March 23, 1991, it really paid off when I scored my first NHL goal.

We were facing off against the Flyers in Philadelphia that night, and it was a wild one. We ended up losing that game 7–4, but the excitement of that first goal had me buzzing through the entire game. It wasn't a highlight-reel goal, but it was my style—the result of hard work and good teamwork. Bernie Nicholls carried the puck into the Flyers' zone and then left a drop pass for Brian Leetch, who threw the brakes on just inside the Philadelphia blue line. I used my speed to sneak in behind the Flyers, and Leetch, who saw me streaking in, fed me a perfect pass. All I had to do was put my stick on the ice and I had an easy tap-in.

I'd been waiting my whole life for that moment—the chance to celebrate my first goal in the big leagues with my teammates around me. The guys on the team were excited about it, too. The older guys on the Rangers had told me it didn't matter where we were playing or what the score was, they wanted me to ride my stick after I scored my first goal. The move was a throwback to Dave "Tiger" Williams, who was one of my many idols. He retired from the NHL in 1988 with more penalty minutes than any player in the history of the league. Tiger not only racked up 3,996 PIMs in his career, but he also scored 241 goals. And to celebrate scoring a big goal, Tiger would wedge his stick between his legs, squat down on it, and cruise past centre ice, yelling and pointing at the crowd like a cowboy on his horse.

Being so young, I did what the veterans on the team told me to do. Amazingly, when I celebrated like I did that night in Philadelphia, nobody on the Flyers reacted. I was waiting for someone to come at me, but I think they were just in shock because nobody ever did anything like that back then in Philly.

I spent the next summer working hard during the day and enjoying my time in New York at night, and before I knew it, I was back in training camp for the next season. I made the cut again that year, and the season looked like it would pick up right where the last one left off. But then the Rangers' management made a move that meant we were in for a very different season. On October 4,

1991, the Rangers acquired Mark Messier from the Edmonton Oilers. As you can imagine, Messier coming to New York meant a lot to everyone on the team, not just me. Two weeks earlier, he had helped lead Team Canada to a win over the United States in the finals of the Canada Cup. In 1990, he captained the Oilers to their fifth Stanley Cup in seven years. The fact that he managed to do that after Wayne Gretzky had left the Oilers to play with the Los Angeles Kings is even more impressive. Messier was on top of the hockey world, and now he was set to lead us.

Mark's first practice after the trade came while we were on the road in Montreal. The Zamboni was still on the ice when Messier arrived at the bench. He was dressed in entirely new gear except for his classic Winnwell helmet, and he looked immediately comfortable. He didn't even wait for the Zamboni to finish before he stepped onto the ice, and as soon as he did that, everyone else found themselves glued to the bench, just staring at him in awe. I am not kidding when I say this—the whole team was overwhelmed at the mere sight of the guy. So Mess just stood on the ice by himself, stickhandling the puck.

I was a young kid, and there wasn't a teammate I didn't care about. And I was never intimidated by anyone, not even a legend like Messier. So I stepped onto the ice while everyone else waited for the Zamboni to finish. As soon as I got on, Messier fired me a perfect saucer pass. I said to him, "*This* is how you do a real saucer pass," and I sent Messier a pass that wasn't nearly as smooth as his had been. That got him laughing his head off, and it broke the ice—suddenly, all of the other guys snapped out of the spell they were under and started laughing along.

Messier arrived in New York with a career most of us could only dream of. We had a lot of young players on the Rangers at that time, and more than anything, we learned a lot from Messier that year just by watching him. Adam Graves or anyone else who was on that team would tell you the same thing. I remember Graves, when we heard that Messier would be joining us, looking at me and saying that Messier was *the* guy. So if Messier decided he had something to say, we were sure as hell going to listen to him. Mess would always tell me, "Don't think, just play." He'd try to get us out of our heads and to feel the game; that way, we could play smart as well as tough. He taught us that you need to practice the way you play, which showed me how to take the skills I had and use them in new ways. I had always taken pride in my skating ability. I learned how to take that and combine it with the toughness I'd shown as an enforcer, not just to fight, but to deliver big, clean hits that could change a play or even a game.

Messier once told me that superstitions will drive you crazy. If you give in to them while you're young, you can't stop; in fact, all you end up doing is adding to them. Because it was Messier saying that, I listened to him—thank goodness. I can't speak for his other teammates, but I know I tried to take in whatever he told me. And he was right about everything he said. Over the rest of my career, I noticed how many guys drove themselves crazy doing all these superstitious rituals before they played. It taught me that you sometimes can't afford to overthink what you need to do; sometimes you just need to do a job and then be done with it.

Messier's impact on our team that year was huge. We ended up winning the President's Trophy—awarded to the NHL team with the most points at the end of the regular season—in 1992, at the end of his first year in New York. Not only that, but Messier won the Hart Memorial Trophy as the league's most valuable player, and Brian Leetch won the Norris Trophy as the league's top defenceman. We had won 50 games and earned 105 points in the regular season. The year before, the Rangers had won 36 games and finished with 85 points. Needless to say, the impact of Messier on the Rangers was immediate.

But for all the improvement we showed that season, we still lost in the second round of the playoffs to the Pittsburgh Penguins in a six-game series. To make matters worse, we had a 2–1 series lead over the Penguins before losing three straight games. After we were knocked out, we had a team party to mark the end of the season. Messier was in a foul mood, and he grabbed Brian Leetch, Adam Graves—whom we called "Gravey"—and me. He had a limo waiting outside and he wanted to get out of there. He was pissed off that the Penguins had knocked us out of the playoffs, and he was even more pissed off that we were having a team party after we had lost. Messier couldn't stand the thought of celebrating losing. He was a born winner, so he was hard on himself. He wanted to have done better, and he wouldn't let himself relax or celebrate until he'd made that happen. There is a reason Messier was such a successful hockey player. When someone has his kind of proven track record of winning championships, you know it's not by accident. Everything Messier did and said was all about winning. He played and acted like a champion on and off the ice, and he expected all his teammates to do the same.

I understood my role on the Rangers and what it meant to the team, and I tried to be smart about how and when I stepped up. And I looked to Messier as an example of what it meant to be a true leader and how I should treat the people around me. I took his words to heart, and I saw his actions as inspiration for how I could work on my skills and develop myself into a more well-rounded player. It wouldn't happen overnight, but in just one season with the Rangers, Messier had made a lasting difference in my life.

4

Probert

NOBODY TAUGHT me how to be a fighter, or when to fight. I just knew; I always knew. I sensed what to do and when to do it.

I ended up fighting 333 times over the course of my NHL career, and that's not counting Junior C, Junior B, three years of major junior, the minors, preseason and postseason games, and the streets. That is more than any player in the history of the NHL; with the way the game is today, that's a record that will never be broken. Not that I'm proud of it, but it is what it is.

When I was younger, my dad never wanted me to be a fighter. Heck, he never even wanted me to make a living as a hockey player. When I first started playing hockey, he told me, "You better do something else, because hockey isn't going to last forever."

When I broke into the NHL, fighting was a lot different than it is now. Every team had at least one badass enforcer on its roster. I fought 16 times in 42 games in 1991–92, and while that might sound like a lot, I was fighting guys that year like Gino Odjick, Craig Berube, Ken Baumgartner, Marty McSorley, and Rob Ray, all of whom fought a lot more than I did. And they weren't just fighters—they were also in the lineup more than I was that year. I respected each and every one of those guys.

The NHL in the early 1990s wasn't that far removed from the crazy days of the Philadelphia Flyers of the 1970s. When I was a kid, the Broad Street Bullies were feared around the NHL. In the 1974–75 season alone, the Flyers fought 77 times! For years afterward, to keep up with teams like Philly, pretty much every team had a heavyweight who would jump in to protect their team's star players. I remember hearing that in 1996–97 there were 907 fighting majors in the NHL. That sounds about right, because I fought 26 times that year! And I didn't even lead the league in fights that year—I was second to Paul Laus of the Florida Panthers, who was in 39 fights. Nowadays, a tough guy may fight 10–15 times in a season—and usually less than that. And there are very few enforcers in the modern NHL who could compare to the guys that I had to fight when I broke into the league.

Like I said, it was a different league back then. The job I had to do then just doesn't exist anymore. Of my 333 fights, 99 per cent were for my team, to protect my teammates—especially the best players on the team; those were the guys who would win games for you. When I was with the Maple Leafs, any guy coming to Toronto knew that if he hit Mats Sundin, I was going to be coming for him. Some fights were to set the tone of the game by dropping the gloves on the first shift. Other fights were to try to turn the momentum around if we were losing. But every game I laced up for, no matter what dressing room I was in, I was one of the guys in the room who had to react to any situation. I had to be ready, at any given moment in a sixty-minute game, to switch my focus from myself to others, to do my job and assume the responsibility of protecting the people around me. That was just my job as a hockey player. To me, it was less about fighting and more about doing what was right. I am proud of the fact that I *always* protected each and every one of my friends and teammates. I could look every teammate in the eye and know that I never took a shift off or failed to protect him on the ice, and I did it all without regret or a moment's hesitation. I would have done anything to protect the guys on my team. And if that had meant fighting even more than I did, I would have done it. Because next to winning, protecting my team is all that mattered to me. The team always came first.

But there was one fight that was the exception to the rule. A fight that was about making a name for myself and establishing my place among the heavyweights in the NHL. A fight I actually looked forward to.

It was February 9, 1992—only a few weeks after Messier had dressed me down following our game against Buffalo—and the Detroit Red Wings were in town to face us. More important, Bob Probert was coming into Madison Square Garden. Probert was at the top of the list of tough guys back then; he was the undisputed heavyweight champion of the NHL. The year I was drafted into the NHL, Probert had 23 fights, and he won every single time. And he didn't just beat guys; he destroyed them. There had been others before him—John Ferguson Sr. in the 1960s, Dave Schultz and Tiger Williams in the '70s—guys who were tougher and stronger than anyone else in their time. But without question, in the late '80s and early '90s, Probert ruled the league. At six feet, three inches and over 220 pounds, he was the king, a true warrior. Bob Probert was more than just a renowned fighter; he was a heck of a player and one who was feared by everyone in the league.

Bob Probert in his prime in Detroit was probably one of their best players, period. He scored over 20 goals, and when he was on the ice with Steve Yzerman, the Red Wings' best player had a ton of room to work with. Because players feared Probert, they stayed farther away from him than they would from other players, giving Probert that extra second to make a play. I learned how to do the same by watching Probert.

He was the guy I wanted to beat. In fact, I wanted to *be* Probert. I wanted to be the best. But while I certainly respected Bob, because he was the best of the best, I wasn't afraid of him, even though I was just half his size. I was never intimidated by anyone in the NHL—I didn't know any better. I grew up on the street that way, and in the generation I come from, that was the only way to be. You didn't make excuses; if you wanted something, you had to sacrifice for it. I knew the risk of what I was getting into, but up until that point, getting punched in the face had never really hurt me, so why should I be scared to fight anyone? Adam Graves used to wonder why I never got scared. He joked that the word *fear* wasn't a part of my vocabulary. I can't explain why, but it just never entered my mind when I stepped on the ice, no matter who I might be facing that night.

I had tried to fight Probert several times over the years. And every time I had tried, he had turned me down. While he was feared around the league, he wasn't into cheap shots. He was a very honest enforcer. You never feared that Probert was just going to grab you for no reason and pummel you. I respected that about Probie, so I made sure I behaved the same way. I had to persuade him to give me a shot at the title. I would only fight someone like Probert if he agreed to it. I wasn't the kind of player to just jump a guy. I would skate up to a guy, and they would know if they deserved it or not.

SHIFT WORK

That February night in 1992, I sensed that I was finally going to get my chance. I think my Rangers teammates were more nervous than I was that night. The stress of a really big fight was a lot to handle, and I needed to find ways not to think about it. For the first half of my career, I always left a chair in the hallway outside of the dressing room. Often, instead of waiting in the room with the rest of the team before the game, I would go sit in that chair by myself for a little while. When I was in the room, surrounded by my teammates and hearing them talk, my mind went to the game, which meant that it went to fighting. But if I was in the hallway, I could distract myself by talking to the security guards and ushers who passed by. It helped calm me down and keep my mind off of whatever I would need to do on the ice.

On the day of the game against Detroit, I made extra sure that I stayed calm and cool. I didn't want to think about fighting or get too worked up. That was one of my cardinal rules before a game and a fight: be calm. The calmer I was, the better. I was too small to not be in control. Being a shorter player, if I showed any hesitation, I would never have a chance. Throughout my career, whenever I fought big guys, I had to use every advantage and ounce of skill I had in order to make up for a lack of reach. I had to be calmer and smarter. By making sure I was calm going into a fight, I was able to tell myself that I was going to win and that nobody was ever going to beat me.

The fans must have sensed something was going to happen that night, too, because they were buzzing as soon as I stepped onto the ice for my first shift—especially because Probie was already out there. I remember Mark Messier telling me that it was a little bit like Ali versus Frazier. Everybody who came to Madison Square Garden that night expected the fight, so there was an incredible atmosphere in the building, right from the very start. When I finally got on the ice and skated up to Probert at the faceoff dot, the buzz in the arena kicked up a few notches. As we lined up for the faceoff, I leaned in to Probert and said, "Come on, Probie; give me a shot at the title." He didn't budge. He just said, "Get away from me, kid," and chased after the puck.

But I wasn't going to take no for an answer. I kept talking to Probie any time I came near him that shift, trying to convince him to give me a shot. The next time we were both on the ice, I skated up to Probert again and said, "Come on, Probie; let's go." And finally, after all that time, Probert agreed.

This wasn't about protecting any teammate. This fight was about becoming *the* guy in the NHL. Of course, to become the best, I had to win the fight. But as tough as Probert was, I knew I could handle him. I definitely had a strategy on how I was going to fight him.

Probie had nearly half a foot on me, so I knew I had to get inside his extra-long reach. One major advantage I had was my memory. Once I saw something, I never forgot it. I had seen how Probie fought, and I could remember how he liked to punch and that he had a devastating right hand. I could throw punches with both hands, and guys knew that I could hurt them with either one. So in fights, I would often pretend that I was going to start punching with one hand before switching to the other just as the fight started. I would line up in a way that would make the other guy think I was going to throw nothing but lefts, but then I'd switch positions at the last second and start throwing rights, or vice versa. As Probie and I threw down our sticks, I couldn't believe how big of a human he was—on skates, Probert was almost six foot seven. I knew I was going to need everything I had to beat him.

The crowd leapt to its feet as Probert and I squared off over the Rangers logo at centre ice. We didn't waste time. As soon as our gloves were off, Probie and I grabbed hold of each other. It took me a moment to get set, but eventually I got a good grip on his jersey. The Garden was going nuts, but I had no choice but to be calm. Then we started swinging. Probert started out by trying to tag me with some overhand rights. I quickly responded and started throwing lefts. With each punch that I landed, the crowd got louder and louder.

A few seconds into the fight, Probert's helmet went flying, while mine stayed on my big head a little while longer. I worked Probert in circles, ducking and throwing, looking for an opening. One of my favourite tricks in a fight was to duck when guys were throwing punches. Everyone I fought was bigger than me, but when I squatted, I was strong enough to duck and pull at the same time to get them off balance. That would make sure the other guy missed me with his punch, and then, as he tried to get set again, I'd throw a fast bomb. Pull, duck, and throw, all in a single motion. If I tagged a guy with that move, they almost always went down.

Most of my early punches in the fight were left-handed while Probert, as he had a massive height advantage, kept hitting me with those rights. A little later in the fight, after we had traded several punches each, my left skate slipped and I temporarily lost my balance. But I was strong on my skates, and I wasn't going to let this chance literally slip away from me, so I fought to regain my footing quickly. When I slipped, I think Probie thought we were done. But I was just getting started. As soon as I was back up, I saw the shock in Probie's face, and it gave me new energy. I could hear the fans kick it up a notch, so I started throwing lefts again as I used my strength to pull Probert back close to me. My grip on Probie's sweater was so tight that as I pulled myself up, I was able to rip his jersey right off him.

We kept throwing punches back and forth, and then, after nearly a minute of fighting, I found my opening. I kept throwing lefts, and on the fourth shot, I caught Probert with a solid hit that drew blood. I saw right away that I had cut him. Just after that, I switched hands and hit him with a few rights. Finally, after what seemed like an eternity, the linesmen jumped in and broke up the fight. Years later, I saw a website that said Probie and I combined to throw 40 punches in that fight. Typically, I would throw as few punches as possible, usually an average of 10 to 15 in a fight. Not on this night. Probie and I each launched 20 punches at each other.

It wasn't a surprise that, by the time the fight ended, the fans at MSG were going crazy—there's really nothing in the world like the crowd at the Garden. It's hard to describe how loud it was in the rink that night, both during and after the fight. On the way to the penalty box, I forgot for a second the lecture that Messier had given me a few weeks earlier about respecting your peers and respecting the game. This wasn't about the game or the team. My fight with Probert was personal. So on the way to the penalty box, I started miming the World Wrestling Entertainment title belt around my waist, twirling my fingers in the air, cupping my hand to my ear—anything to keep the Garden rocking!

After watching the fight, Joe Cirella shouted, "Holy crap—he just fought Probert!" When the linesmen broke up the fight and I was on my way to the penalty box, Cirella skated over, patted me on the back, and said, "Effing awesome, Tie," before skating back towards the bench. But before he made it there, things got even crazier as a massive line brawl broke out. As I stepped into the box, Cirella started fighting with Steve Chiasson, and at the same time, Gerard Gallant started fighting Paul Broten. None of these guys was a fighter. I sat in the box and watched the show. There were helmets and gloves and sticks scattered all over the ice as the refs tried to get everything back under control. By this point, the crowd was going insane.

After the fight, as I sat in the penalty box, I could tell that some of Probert's Red Wings teammates were stunned to see what had happened. I remember former Detroit forward Keith Primeau telling me once he couldn't believe what he'd just seen. "The immortal had been defeated," Primeau said. "I don't think any of us ever expected to see Bob lose a fight. We thought Probert couldn't lose."

* * *

I am not a boxer, but I know there are boxers who haven't fought half as much as I have. I can't count how many fights I've been in, whether on or off the ice. But despite all the fights, cuts, and bruises, I never took anything to relieve the pain. I had a trainer tell me once that he had never seen a player with such a high pain threshold. I don't know why I was that way; I just was. I could take a punch and a hit and a slash and keep coming at you. I didn't need to take anything after the game. It wasn't that stuff wasn't available in the dressing room if I needed it. A lot of guys would take things like Toradol to deal with the pain of an injury, a blocked shot, or a fight. But I never wanted or needed to take painkillers or anything like that. Whenever I got stitches, I refused to let the doctors give me anything beforehand to dull the pain. It wasn't that I wanted to prove how tough I was—I just hate needles and the sight of blood. So instead, I would just close my eyes and force myself to sit still as I felt every stitch the doctors put in me.

In the games following my faceoff against Probert, I had plenty more fights. From the moment that I cut Probert through the end of my career, everybody hit me with their best shot—or tried to—and wanted to take my head off. It's not the ideal way for your kids to see you make a living, but it was a part of my job, and I chose to do it.

71

After that first fight with Probie, everyone was wondering when there would be a rematch. Well, ten months later we were scheduled to face the Red Wings at Madison Square Garden again. Of course, everyone—the fans and the media—assumed this was the night for Round 2. The league president, Gil Stein, was so concerned that he had Probert and me come into his office the night before the game. He told us that if we fought each other again, we would both be suspended twenty games, slapped with hefty fines—you name it. Well, as we lined up for our first shift, the crowd was already going nuts. Probie skated up to me and said, "Tie, let's get it over with."

"Probie, don't you remember the meeting we had yesterday with the president?" I asked.

"No, let's just get it over with," he responded.

The puck dropped, and Probert just started slugging away at me. He must have been pretty pissed off about the last time we fought, because he really meant business that night in New York. At first, it was all I could do to hang on. But after Probert landed a few punches, I regained my rhythm and started throwing lefts. The fight just went on and on until I fell down at the end. I didn't go down because of any punch from Probert; I was just so exhausted at the end of the fight that I could barely stand anymore, and he was so big. Somebody told me afterwards that they couldn't keep track of how many punches Probert threw that night. They lost count after forty. Probie and I ended up fighting fifteen times over the course of my career, but I think this was the fight where Probert realized he couldn't hurt me. He tried as hard as he could that night, but he just couldn't do it.

Even though we were both in the NHL at the same time for eleven seasons, Probert and I rarely got the chance to speak with each other. It wasn't until years later, when Probert got a job on CBC's *Battle of the Blades*, that we finally got the chance to connect.

When the creators of the show first approached me about being on *Battle of the Blades*, I told them the only way I would do it is if they made Probert, not just me, the face of the show. The film company was reluctant because of Probie's past and his criminal record. But I really wanted to involve the guy who had given me my shot; he had given me an opportunity, and I wanted to repay the favour. So I held my ground, and eventually they came back around. When they agreed to take Bob, I joined the show.

Probert and I spent a lot of time talking about our hockey days, and he was completely honest with me about our fights. He said that I was the toughest guy he had ever fought and that my punches were the hardest he was ever hit with. I knew he meant it, because he said it to my face. When you receive praise like that from someone you admire, it's humbling.

Probert and I stayed close even after the show finished. I quickly realized that Probert was a special guy. I know why guys loved him; he was like a big teddy bear, and he had the funniest laugh. I introduced Probie to my friends, my family, even my hairdresser, Santino. Santino, in particular, loved Probie. As soon as Bob met someone, he was their best friend.

One of my favourite memories of Bob is of the U2 concert we attended in Toronto during the taping of *Battle of the Blades*. I took the whole cast of the show to the concert, and the stage attendants brought us right to the front. Bob was like a little kid that night. He was on his cell phone with his family, holding his phone up to the speaker so they could hear the concert. Probert's wife and kids were everything to him. I got to know Bob as a person, and regardless of what people said or thought about him, he was a man I greatly respected. Everyone has their opinions, but I was impressed by Bob. I know he wasn't perfect, but who is? Everyone makes mistakes. When it came down to it, he took care of his teammates on the ice and of his family off of it.

It was a real eye-opener and a reality check when Probert passed away in the middle of the lake with his family in July 2010. You think about him, and it takes you back to all the other enforcers who played before and after him. We all had the same job, and we all faced the same danger every night as we stepped on the ice. I feel lucky that I was able to spend a lot of quality time with Bob and that I really got to know him. He was a sweet guy. Probie and I had some special moments, both on and off the ice. He gave me a chance to become the player I was, and he helped me make a name for myself in my career, which to this day is something that I'm still known for. I will never forget our battles on the ice and what they did for me. But more than that, I will be forever grateful I had the privilege of getting to know the man himself.

5

Lessons from a Hot Tub

A S MUCH as the Probert fight raised my profile, it was also the start of a lot of my troubles. I had worked hard to keep my life outside the rink separate from my career on it. I had trained myself to leave a fight behind me when I went home after a game, and I developed strategies to keep the work I did from weighing on me. But suddenly, I couldn't go anywhere without being brought back to my match against Probert. Teammates talked about it, sports highlight shows replayed it, and everyone on the street was buzzing about it. There was even a full-page story about me and that fight in the *New York Times*. I couldn't escape the reminders.

But the worst of it came when I was out at night. Guys would see me in the bar or on the street—big guys. They would have a few drinks in them, and all of a sudden they'd get brave. It was worse when I was out with girls when I was single; that seemed to always give guys an excuse to cause a scene. One night, I was out at a bar with some teammates after a game when one of those sorts of guys started staring me down from across the bar. I tried to ignore him and enjoy my time with the people around me, but he made his way over to the bar and started smoking right beside me. He took a long puff on his cigarette and then turned and blew the smoke all over me. It was clear this guy had had a few drinks, so I tried to let it pass.

"Hey, come on," I said, trying to move away.

"What?" he said. "What are you going to do?"

Then he reached out and rubbed the short hair on my head, as if I were his pet.

"If you blow smoke on me or touch me again," I warned him, "I will knock you out."

The guy looked down at me and laughed as he turned away, and I thought that was the end of it. But only a minute later, he took another drag of his cigarette, turned, and blew it all over me and the girls around me. I didn't say anything. I turned around, threw one punch, and knocked him out cold. My teammates were all there, but by the time they turned to look at me, all they saw was the guy on the ground.

I didn't want that kind of attention, and I didn't want to have to deal with those sorts of guys. Luckily, I found myself with a crew of teammates who supported me through that time. At the time, I was sharing an apartment with Adam Graves. Adam and I had originally met when I was playing Junior B in Windsor and he was playing with the major junior team the Spitfires. Although I was a year younger than Adam, he had a reputation as one of the nicest guys in hockey (almost too nice!), so we were pretty much friends right from the start, and it was natural that we would become roommates during my time with the Rangers. On top of that, both Tony Amonte and Doug Weight—two US college hockey stars— lived across from Adam and me in the same town house complex.

Because the four of us were young guys living and playing hockey together in New York, we bonded quickly. We became a tight-knit crew, and we watched each other's backs through more than a few scrapes.

One night in Chicago, we had a run-in with two strangers. They were really drunk and obnoxious, and they decided they needed to push someone around to prove they were tough. They were picking on Amonte and Weight, and they had their fingers in their faces to threaten them. That's when I tapped the two drunk guys on the shoulder.

"Hey, what are you doing? Get your fingers out of my friends' faces," I said.

They turned around and shoved their fingers in my face. Before they knew what was happening, I had grabbed both of them by their throats, pushed them over to the stairs, and tossed them down. Joey Kocur was standing behind me the whole time. Lucky for these guys, they had to deal with me instead of him. We were all young, but we knew how to carry ourselves. And if they didn't know it before, Amonte and Weight knew I had their backs after that night.

I couldn't seem to keep away from trouble. But it was around that time that I met and became friends with a veteran New York City police detective, Gus Cecchini, or "Cheech" as I called him. Because I was being targeted after games, whenever I went out with anyone from the team, we would ask Cheech to tag along to take care of us when he was off duty and out of uniform. If it looked like someone was going to start some trouble, Cheech would just step in, which quieted things down in a real hurry. I needed someone like Cheech watching out for me. Doing what I had to do on the ice, the last thing I needed was to get into fights off it. In Cheech, I had one more person watching my back when I went out with the boys in New York. Since then, I've always tried to repay Cheech and his family for what he has done for me. The only times I've ever gotten into any kind of argument with Cheech involved who was paying the cheque.

Thanks to the people I had around me, that scrape with the guy who blew smoke on me was the last fight I ever had off the ice. And eventually, things began to quiet down, letting me focus on hockey again. Wayne Cashman was one of the assistant coaches with the Rangers while I was there, and he meant a lot to me as a young player. He knew what I was going through because he had experienced similar battles himself back in the 1970s with the Big Bad Bruins. So Cash would constantly screw around with me to keep me calm. That helped me get my mind off of fighting so that I could focus on helping the team in other ways. Our coach at that time was Roger Neilson, and he was great at helping us develop as players. Before each game, he would write quick headlines for each player on the opposing team and what their tendencies were. This was my kind of studying. His notes were great—they were short and it was easy to understand what he was getting at. That process was helping me become a smarter player, and I was excited to be focusing on how to be a better hockey pro again.

Then my world came to a stop. It was the end of a Wednesday night at Madison Square Garden, and I had had a great game. In fact, it was one of my best games up to that point in my career. I was feeling great in the dressing room, but after I'd gotten out of my gear, Roger pulled me into his office. My first thought was that I was going to be sent down to the minors. I didn't see how that was possible, considering how good a game I'd had. Instead, Roger dropped the worst bomb anyone could possibly imagine. He simply said, "Your father passed away tonight at eight thirty p.m." My dad had been watching me play on TV while playing cards and drinking coffee with his buddies back in the Junction in Toronto when he'd passed away suddenly.

I arrived home the next day from New York, and when I walked into my parents' house, I saw my sister, Trish, lying on the couch. I told her, "Don't worry, I'm going to take care of you." With my dad gone, I realized we were all going to have to be there for each other more than ever. So from that moment on, I did everything I possibly could to take care of Trish and everyone else in my family. We couldn't and wouldn't let ourselves just drift apart. That's not what my dad would have wanted. We were heartbroken and in mourning, and the suddenness of my dad's passing away was hard to take, but we still had our lives to live and people around us we had to take care of. To keep ourselves on track and to take care of my mom, we would have to remember what Dad taught us and do whatever it takes to figure things out.

* * *

After my dad died, I hoped I would have some time with my family to sort things out and pull myself back together. But life didn't slow down. Nothing lasts forever, and sure enough, my time in New York City was about to come to an end. In December 1992 I was traded to the Winnipeg Jets. I had heard some rumours that I might be dealt. I wasn't playing, so I asked our general manager, Neil Smith, to be traded. I told him he could trade me anywhere; my only request was to not be sent to Winnipeg. My mom didn't want me to move there because she thought it was too cold. So of course, on December 28, 1992, where did I get traded but to Winnipeg. I learned early to be careful what you ask for.

In hindsight, I don't hold any grudge against Neil for trading me to the Jets. After all, Neil was the reason I had been brought to New York in the first place. But at the time, I wasn't quite so accepting about the whole thing. Leaving the bright lights and the big city of Manhattan for Winnipeg wasn't something I was thinking of or hoping for. And to have to change teams halfway through the season was tough. I had been making a life for myself in New York that I was enjoying, and after my dad's death, I didn't like the idea of moving farther away from my family.

When it happened, I could have sulked. I could have caused a scene. But my dad's words and lessons came into play; after he passed away, I noticed that I was hearing his voice in my head even more than usual. My dad had always found a way to make things work and be positive, regardless of the situation, and I was determined to do the same. As I packed up my stuff from our house, Gravey and I talked about what Winnipeg might mean for me. He helped me realize that the move was actually an opportunity, not a setback. Starting over in Winnipeg was just another challenge, and, like everything else in my life, I had to take it on.

So, as much as I didn't want to be traded to Winnipeg, I told myself the town could be as good to me as New York had been. Playing a much more prominent role with the Jets than I had with the Rangers would allow me to take my career to another level. I always say that there are no rearview mirrors in life. So I didn't sulk—I pulled myself together and turned my sights to Winnipeg.

It didn't take long after arriving in Winnipeg to realize what an opportunity was ahead of me. That became clear as soon as I met Teemu Selänne. He and I pretty much bonded right away. He might have been a rookie, but he knew why the Jets had traded for me: I was there to protect him and let him do his thing. And Teemu's thing was scoring goals. It worked, too, because that year Teemu ended up breaking Mike Bossy's record for goals scored by a rookie. Actually, Teemu didn't break the record; he shattered it—he netted 76 goals that year, 23 more than Bossy had scored as a rookie in 1977–78. He was just that good.

Guys who played against Teemu on the ice said that, when he decided to take off, it was as if he was shot out of a cannon. His breakaway speed was amazing. Once he got moving, there weren't many players in the league who had any chance of catching him. He was special.

I can still remember the night that Selänne broke Bossy's record. It's one of my favourite memories from my time in the NHL. It was March 2, 1993, and we were playing the Quebec Nordiques at the old Winnipeg Arena. The Nordiques had a shot that was steered wide of the net. The puck rattled around the boards and came to me on the right wing, down low in our end. I took a few strides out of our zone and flipped the puck up high in the air to Selänne, and he did the rest. Selänne easily outraced the poor Nordiques defenceman for the puck. Stéphane Fiset, the Nordiques' goalie, had come out of his net to play the puck, but Selänne beat him to it and, before Fiset knew it, had buried the puck for his record-setting 54th goal of the year. Just after he scored, Selänne tossed his glove high in the air and pretended to shoot it with his stick as if he were duck hunting. That's still one of the cockiest goal celebrations you'll ever see. At this point, everyone in the arena was going absolutely nuts. We all mobbed Selänne to help him celebrate the goal, and the fans wouldn't stop cheering. Honestly, as his teammates, we were just as excited as Teemu was. It was an incredible moment for an incredible guy.

While protecting Teemu was my main job in Winnipeg, I sensed that something was missing with the Jets when I arrived. The dressing room wasn't close; it seemed like everyone was on their own island. We had Russians, Swedes, Czechs, Finns, Americans, Canadians—you name it—on the team. I knew I would have to do something to bring everybody together.

So, two days after I arrived in Winnipeg, I decided to call a team party. My girlfriend at the time, Leanne, and I were living in an apartment that was the size of a closet. Despite the limited space, I managed to convince Leanne that I had to bring a hot tub into the apartment to liven the party up. Leanne and I were young, so we thought, what the hell? I figured if I rented a hot tub and found a way to get it into our apartment, we could do some real team bonding. Looking back, I am still amazed we were able to get that hot tub into the building. The thing ended up taking up an entire bedroom, but we made it fit. And it was worth it. The party was a big hit with everyone and helped bring the team together by having the guys get to know each other outside of what they did on the ice. Teemu was the last one to leave the party, with the exception of one teammate, defenceman Freddie Olausson. That was because Freddie was passed out in the bathtub.

It may seem crazy, but the hot tub party was inspired by the lessons in leadership that Messier had taught me in New York: everybody on the team is equal and everybody has an important role to play. I knew that if we were going to have a chance of being a winner in Winnipeg, we had to be a team, both on and off the ice. And that only happens when you know that the guys in the dressing room have your back, no matter what situation you're in.

I didn't want the new team chemistry we'd found at the party to just fade away. I always felt there was more to being a team than just throwing a bunch of talented guys together in a room. Everyone needed to know that we were all in it together and that everyone had each other's back. And that didn't just mean Canadian guys sticking up for other Canadian guys. I made it clear to every player that it didn't matter where they were from or what language they spoke, we were teammates. So over the next few weeks, I paid attention to the little things to make sure that the guys kept getting along. We had a few Russians on the team, and to make them feel more welcome, I started singing Russian songs with them in the dressing room shower. They loved it. They had never had a North American player sing with them like that before. I also learned how to swear in almost every language that guys spoke in the dressing room. I picked up all the worst words from a bunch of different languages over the years—Russian, Swedish, Czech, Finnish— and it was always a fun way to bond with the guys from different countries. I couldn't actually speak those languages, but because of my good memory and because I heard the words so often, I was able to remember them. It was helpful on the ice, too. I would really freak out Russian guys on other teams when I would swear at them in the middle of games in their own language. They would look at me like I had ten heads.

We went on a pretty good run to cap off the 1992–93 season. We went 9-3-1 over the last 13 games to finish at 40-37-7. When I was traded from the Rangers, New York had been in a playoff spot, while Winnipeg was sitting on the outside, looking in. Coincidentally, after I got traded to Winnipeg, we managed to make the playoffs, while the Rangers missed out. Not bad for a young team that was rebuilding. Still, the following year, the Rangers won the

Cup. It's funny; when I think back on my time with the Rangers, I could dwell on the fact that I missed out on winning a Stanley Cup with them in 1994 because I'd asked to be traded. But I don't think that way. Sure, if I hadn't been traded, I might have won a Cup in New York, but that wouldn't replace all the experiences I had as a hockey player in my career. If I'd stayed in New York, I would have been just a fighter. With the trade to Winnipeg, I got to become a player. Nothing else could ever substitute for all of the experiences I've had, the people I've met, or the teammates I've gotten to know.

* * *

In my next season with the Jets, we picked up right where we left off, kicking off the season 6-3-1 over our first 10 games. But we couldn't keep up the pace, and we ended the season with the second-worst record in the league. I played 81 games that year, scoring 8 goals and getting 11 assists for 19 points. I also ended up with 347 penalty minutes. Although I retired with 3,515 penalty minutes in my career, I only led the league in PIMs in one year—that 1993–94 season I spent with the Jets. That same year I was named the Jets' most popular player, as voted by the fans. But my personal contributions didn't change our team's record, and so the year finished with us out of the playoffs.

Even though we had a tough, losing season, playing with Teemu Selänne was still an incredible experience. I was very fortunate to play with some great players over the course of my career, and Teemu is right there towards the top of that list. Selänne was not only a great player, but a great person. He was always joking. Selänne was such a gifted player, but he never acted like he was special. He always carried himself like he was just another player on the team, and he genuinely loved being around everyone. He was the sort of guy you wanted to protect, and I felt like we had a long road ahead of us as teammates.

The 1994–95 season began with the NHL locking out the players. It took three months for the owners and the players' association to reach an agreement, and on January 11, 1995, it was back to business as usual. I was now in my third season with Winnipeg, and despite some setbacks in the standings, I felt like we were building a team with the potential to have a lot of success in the years to come. I also assumed I was going to be in Winnipeg for a while. But as I said, the life of a pro sports athlete can change anytime.

One night, in late March 1995, we were playing the Leafs in Winnipeg in the back end of a home-and-home series with Toronto. There was a faceoff in the neutral zone, in front of the Leafs' bench, and I skated up to take my place at right wing. As I was waiting for the puck to drop, I heard someone on the bench say something to me. I turned around to find Pat Burns, the Leafs' coach at the time, looking at me. He repeated it so I could hear him:

"No, seriously, I'd love to have you on my right side."

Sure enough, less than two weeks later, on April 7, the Leafs picked me up in a trade-deadline deal. I couldn't believe it. Burns and the Leafs had sent Mike Eastwood and a third-round pick to the Jets to bring me back to Toronto to play on the right side for the Leafs, just as Burns had said.

Looking back, I wish I could have played more games with Teemu—I only ended up playing a total of 161 games with the Jets. Despite initially telling Neil Smith I would be willing to be traded anywhere *but* Winnipeg, I ended up enjoying my time there. When I think about it, Neil had actually done me a big favour. Being in Winnipeg allowed me to form a lifelong friendship with Teemu Selänne, and it allowed me to start a family. Leanne and I ended up getting married, and our first two kids were born in Winnipeg—my son, Max, actually only lived in Winnipeg for less than a month before we moved to Toronto.

Playing for Winnipeg had also caused my reputation around the league to change. Coaches and general managers saw what I could do on the ice with Teemu and the guys in Winnipeg, and so they started to look at me as not just a fighter, but as a more complete hockey player. Just like Gravey had told me as I was leaving New York, my time with the Jets had been an opportunity. By making the best of it, I had improved my career and created options for myself. I had learned a lot about what it means to be a team player and a leader, and at the end of the day, it turned out that playing for the Winnipeg Jets was good for me and for my family. And now the trade to Toronto had brought me back, full circle, to the team that drafted me.

Plus, I learned that you can fit a hot tub into a small apartment for a team party.

6

Good Cop, Bad Cop

WHEN I arrived at Maple Leaf Gardens to rejoin the Leafs, Pat Burns immediately called me into his office for a meeting. As I sat down across from him, the first thing he said to me was, "I told you I wanted you on my right side." Then he got deadly serious about what he expected from me. "I brought you here to make you into a hockey player. I know how tough you are. I was a cop. I know about people who protect others. I need you to protect this big Swede. Because he's special, he's really special."

Burns also told me something he would repeat to the rest of the team all the time: "If you play hard, I will reward you." As any athlete knows, when you hear those words from a coach—that if you give it your best and play hard every shift, you'll get rewarded—it's music to your ears. I never took a shift off my whole career. I didn't know what that was. I only knew one way to play, and that was all-out on every shift. So when Pat Burns said what he did, I knew I was in the right place. Burns knew I was a decent hockey player, and he knew how tough I was. And now he wanted me to bring the toughness I'd shown in Winnipeg to Toronto. He told me, "If you play every game, you play hard, and you play hurt, you'll not only own this city, you'll own this country."

He went on to say, "I want to see you leading in the locker room, not lying on a trainer's table." It was his way of telling me he didn't want me to be like some other players who spent their time getting treated for even the smallest injury. These were the sort of guys who would hold back in practice or who would milk their injuries. I had seen veterans in the minors like that, and I didn't want to be one of those guys. I took everything Pat Burns said to heart, especially his advice about needing to tough it out through an injury. So I ended up getting my own therapists and doing a lot of my treatment at home. The chiropractors I hired myself were the best. I never wanted to show anyone on the team, especially the coaches, that I was hurt, and I would never admit to being in pain or needing treatment. I would never have played half of the games that I did if I didn't play hurt. I didn't want to let my teammates down, and if I wasn't in the lineup, it meant opponents could take advantage of my teammates. It was my job to protect my teammates, just like it had been to protect my friends on the street as a kid. I always stick up for people that I work with. And I wouldn't let anything, least of all my own pain and injuries, get in the way of doing my job.

It didn't take long practising and playing for Burns before I knew that he was, by a mile, the best coach I had ever had up to that point. Like me, he was a street guy, so he could relate to me and the way I was. A lot of guys who played for Pat talked about "the look." Sometimes Pat would just stare at a guy to let him know he wasn't happy or that he didn't like something the player had done during a game. He didn't need to say anything; his look said it all. I guess I never pissed off Pat, because he never gave me that look. He respected my job and what I did, and I respected him and his methods in return.

Before our first practice, Pat said to me, "Give me everything you got. My practices are short and high-tempo. If you give me all you have and you empty the tank, by the end you will be tired. But you'll be more effective and you will be a better player." We would practice for forty to forty-five minutes at a high tempo and then we would be done. That approach was unusual at the time, but other coaches are finally starting to do it his way now. In that way, Pat was ahead of his time. And he was the one coach who challenged me every day to be a better player. He told me time and again how tough I was, but more than that, he showed me how to take that to the next level. I was like a project to Pat. He was determined to make me more than just a fighter. He believed that I could be a more complete player if I was willing to listen to him. He always kept on me—he was hard on me, but I knew he did it because he cared and wanted me to succeed. That made all the difference in my career. The way that Burns treated me and talked to me made me realize that I didn't have to prove anything to him. Pat was true to his word. I did play hard every shift for him and the harder I worked, the more I played. The more I played, the more I learned, and the better I became. Slowly but surely, Pat made me a hockey player.

Things moved fast once I joined the Leafs. My first game with the Leafs was the same day I got traded from Winnipeg: April 7, against the Detroit Red Wings at the Gardens. That was also the day that I met the big, shy Swede that Pat had been talking about, a guy named Mats Sundin.

The first time I got on the ice with Mats at practice, I could tell he was special. As it turned out, he was a Hall of Fame kind of special. He was a big guy, but he moved so smoothly on the ice. And here is something you have to understand—when you're the guy whose job it is to protect skilled guys like Mats, Teemu, and Mark those guys are often very loyal in return. Just like Selänne, Mats recognized that, so he and I became close friends almost right away. Before you knew it, we were basically doing everything together. I took my job seriously, so when Burns asked me to take care of Mats, I made sure to do it, both on and off the ice. Mats would do anything for me, and I would do anything for him. Because I knew right away that if Mats was protected and was allowed to do his thing, we would win a lot of games.

It paid off almost right away. Just one month later, on May 7, we faced the Chicago Blackhawks in Game 1 of our opening-round playoff series. A few short days after that, on May 17, it was Game 6 of that same series and we were facing elimination. Our season was close to done that night, but we pulled out a 5–4 win over the Blackhawks to force a seventh and deciding game. What I remember more than any play during the game, though, was walking through the old Chicago Stadium afterwards. Instead of the usual energy and noise that follows a playoff game, the place was subdued and quiet; you could hear a pin drop. The feeling of winning such a big game in the loudest stadium in the league was incredible. It was a thrill to silence the Chicago crowd, because they had been so sure they were going to beat us that night. It was a totally different feeling from what I'd had in Winnipeg, and I couldn't wait to see where we could take it from there. Unfortunately, we couldn't close the deal that series, and in Game 7, the Blackhawks beat us 5–2 to win it. But even though our season was over, I'd seen the sort of skill and grit we could show when we came together as a team, and I was determined to help us become serious contenders.

So I threw myself into my role. I protected Mats in the pre-season, in the regular season, and in the postseason. For all his abilities, during his first year in Toronto, Mats just didn't have the same kind of supporting cast as other superstars. Mario Lemieux had Jaromir Jagr. Wayne Gretzky had had Mark Messier. In the modern game, you have Patrick Kane and Jonathan Toews in Chicago, and Evgeni Malkin and Sidney Crosby in Pittsburgh. You need someone to complement your best player, and there had been many nights where it seemed like Mats was expected to do it all by himself. In his prime, Mats never really had that support, which made it easy for other teams to target him and shut him down. But once I arrived, everyone who played the Leafs knew what would happen to them if they tried to hurt Mats. In my time with Toronto, nobody ever got Mats with a really bad cheap shot, and if they tried, I made sure they paid for it. The worst injury that Mats ever received was from our own teammate, Bryan McCabe, who hit him in the face with a pass.

And it wasn't just Mats; everyone in the league knew that if a player did anything to any of my teammates, I was coming and they had better be ready to answer the bell. I always understood the role that I needed to play and what was expected from me. I was being paid to play hard, defend my teammates, and be a leader. And to me, being a leader in the NHL meant leading by example and letting the way I did my job do the talking.

In our time with the Leafs, Mats and I would sit beside each other on flights and bus rides to the rink. Eventually, it got to the point where we would have breakfast and dinner together pretty much every time we were on the road. Even though he was the most skilled guy on the team, he made everyone feel equal and was always humble in everything he did. Right from day one, I teased Mats about everything. No matter how much I grilled him about stuff, though, it never bothered him. He would always laugh it off. When your best player can laugh at himself, it makes everyone else feel comfortable.

I never understood how, when we were on the road, guys could stay in their rooms to order room service. Mats and I made a point of eating out when we were on the road and invited anyone else on the team who wanted to join us. Some guys understood where we were coming from. Even as a player, Gary Roberts was a nutrition fanatic. He was always fighting me to not eat any bread. I didn't listen at the time, but if I'd known then that I had a gluten intolerance, I sure would have! The one time I would use room service, though, was for dessert. If a hotel had Häagen-Dazs ice cream, I'd order a container of vanilla ice cream to my room, and Mats would join me. We had it down to a science. Vanilla ice cream with chocolate sauce on the side—that was our go-to. We would eat some of the vanilla out of the top of the container and then start pouring the chocolate sauce in and eating the whole thing right out of the bucket. And I am talking about a whole container of Häagen-Dazs. Can you imagine doing that now, with the focus on nutrition in the league? We did it every trip—it got to the point where we tried to have the team book hotels that served Häagen-Dazs. That was our ritual the night before games.

In spending so much time together over food, Mats and I ended up getting to know someone else who has now been a dear friend of mine for years: Ted Nikolaou. Ted opened Harbour Sixty—the best steak house in North America—at the same time that the Air Canada Centre opened in 1999, and he sat behind our bench for years. Mats and I went to Harbour Sixty almost every day we were in Toronto, whether we were having lunch with Ted or not. Ted is the epitome of old school. He came to Canada with nothing and started out shining shoes. One night, after a Leafs-Habs game at the ACC, I had dinner at Harbour Sixty with Mark Wahlberg. It was a Saturday night and the place was packed. Mark had an amazing amount of respect for Ted and how he'd made so much success for himself, so he called over to one of the waiters — "Waiter, throw me a towel!" By this time, the whole place was watching as Mark walked over to Ted, holding the towel. Mark bent down on one knee, picked up Ted's shoes, and started shining them right then and there. As he was doing it, Mark said, loud enough for everyone to hear, "Anybody who started shining shoes and built a place like this deserves to have his own shoes shined in his own place."

Mats and I had great respect for Ted, so whenever he talked, we listened. Ted once told me that it isn't about where you came from; what matters is where you end up and who is with you along the way. Sitting there with Mats, knowing that we both wanted to win a championship and that we wanted to win it together, Ted's words couldn't have been more fitting.

Mats helped me to become more of a leader with the Leafs. I once told him that it wasn't his job to deal with every single problem that guys on the team might have. Mats didn't have the time; he had to focus on being the best player on the team, and later, as captain, he had to talk to the media every day, win or lose. With Mats handling that kind of responsibility, it was *my* job to deal with all the different backgrounds and personalities and egos in the dressing room, to make sure every other player was taken care of. He had his role and I had mine, and the better I was at my job, the more time Mats had to concentrate on his game being the best.

Not that I minded doing it. I was a sociable guy—I always have been—so in my first full year with the Leafs, I became the "fine-master" on the team. We had a number of things that would get you fined back then—things like being late for meetings, buses, or planes—and I would collect any fines the guys had to pay. And if a guy didn't pay within seven days, the fine would double. At the end of the year, we would use the money to throw a big team party. Sometimes we had enough money for two parties over two nights—the first night with just the guys, and the second night with everyone's girlfriends and wives.

I made sure to include all the trainers and equipment guys in the parties. They were a key part of the team, and I always felt it was important to take care of everyone on the team, not just the players. As a kid, I had watched my dad treat people of every background the same way, and it has never occurred to me to do anything different. I liked keeping the whole team close. The guys who steered off on their own were the jealous ones, and they knew that if they didn't get with the program, they wouldn't last long. I knew who was who. I'd experienced that throughout junior and in the other cities I'd played in the NHL, and I didn't want to have it happen again, so when I got to Toronto and Mats and I were given the reins, we started to do things our way.

* * *

It was during my time playing for Pat Burns that my infamous incident with Ulf Samuelsson happened. By now, everyone has seen the video a thousand times. The quick summary is that I knocked out Samuelsson with one punch, and I ended up getting suspended eight games for it. I deserved it. But that doesn't tell the whole story.

It was October 14, 1995, and we were playing Samuelsson and the Rangers at Maple Leaf Gardens. It was our third game of the year, a Saturday night—*Hockey Night in Canada*, Bob Cole, Ron MacLean, Don Cherry, all of it. It was a big matchup, and that meant a lot of people were watching what happened.

Ulf and I had been tangled in the corner, and when we got back in the play, he wouldn't let go of my stick. I was standing in front of the Rangers' net, and Samuelsson kept right on me, doing whatever he could to distract me and get me out of position. If he'd stuck to pushing me around, nothing would have happened. I was used to that kind of play. Ulf played hard, but I knew he'd never fight me. But the entire time we were battling for position, Ulf kept saying to me, "Come on, dummy," along with plenty of worse things. I tried to block him out, but he'd been chirping me over and over. I don't think he realized how angry he was making me. Samuelsson was always egging me on to try to draw a penalty. I think he figured that if he kept doing it, I would slash him or cross-check him and take a two-minute minor.

Well, he said, "Come on, dummy," one too many times. I threw one punch, straight to his face, and knocked him out cold.

I was kicked out of the game. My night was over, but the fallout didn't end there. Only a day or two later, the league handed me an eight-game suspension for the incident. They thought my actions were too aggressive, and they wanted to set an example to show that they wouldn't let that kind of behaviour slide. Brian Burke was the head of league discipline at the time, and he was going to suspend me a lot longer than eight games. But I insisted on telling my side of the story about what had happened that night and why I'd done it. I didn't want to be known as a guy who would sucker punch guys or throw cheap shots. Afterwards, Burke said he was glad that

I told him the whole story. Ultimately, though, it didn't change the league's decision—I was still suspended for eight games.

After the suspension, the question everyone had about the incident was why I did it. I did it because Samuelsson called me a dummy. Lots of guys had tried to trash talk me throughout my career to rattle me, and most of the time, it had no effect on me. Most of their insults were about the size of my head, which was a pretty obvious target. But I was sensitive about what Ulf said. I thought he was making fun of my family name and of things I'd struggled with since I was a kid, and his words got to me. Ulf's insult was the straw that broke the camel's back. Still, I knew right away that I shouldn't have reacted the way I did.

Luckily, Burns had my back through the entire thing. As tough and intimidating as Pat Burns could be, there was another side to him that not everyone got to see. Pat could be spitting mad and yelling at you one day, and then the next day turn into the happiest guy ever as he gave you a hug. I mostly saw the forgiving, supportive Pat, as I did after the Samuelsson incident. But later that season, in a game against Chicago, there was a line brawl, five on five, and I got tangled up with Chris Chelios. We both had our gloves off, but instead of diving right into the fight, I paused. I was squaring off against the most talented player on the other team—there was no way I was going to start pounding him just for the sake of it. Like I said, I never fought a guy unless he was willing to drop the gloves and the fight would serve a purpose. So I said to Chelios, "Chelly, what are you doing?" I was holding on to him with my arm cocked back, ready to hit him, and he looked at me and said, "I don't know." So I let him go.

Chelios was one of the best defencemen in the league. There was no need for me to fight him. If I'd started beating up Chelios,

I wouldn't have felt good about it. But Pat didn't see things the same way as I did that night. When we were in the dressing room at the intermission, Burnsie lost it on me. He dressed me down in front of the entire team, shouting, "You had him at the tip of your fingers, and you let him off the hook!" He was livid.

The next day, we were back in Toronto when one of the trainers came up to me and said, "Burnsie wants to see you." I went into Pat's office, expecting the worst. But as I opened the door, I found Pat halfway through getting changed into his track suit, sitting there by himself with nothing but his white boxer shorts on. I knew he was comfortable around me, but this was a new level. He smiled at me and said, "Hey, what you did last night . . ." As he said it, he stood up to give me a hug. He went on to say, "I'm glad you didn't do what I snapped at you for not doing. Chelios is one of my favourites that I've coached, and you showed a lot of respect."

That meant a lot to me; it told me we spoke the same language, and I understood that Pat didn't mean what he'd said the night before in Chicago. What was I going to do—beat the shit out of Chris Chelios? He was the best player on the Blackhawks, and beating him up wouldn't have been any help to my team. It is not in my DNA to do something like that, and that's not how I looked at the game.

*   *   *

My time playing under Burns was short, but sweet. In March 1996, he was fired by the Leafs. I remember Pat calling me afterwards. I was one of only a handful of people he called after he got the news—our captain, Doug Gilmour, and Burns's kids were among the others. I was upset when I heard the news, but I didn't really know the whole story at the time. I later found out that he had a lot of issues with other players going on that I never knew about. As we finished our call, Pat told me, "Be careful, and take care of yourself. Watch your back." I knew what he was talking about—there had been people in management and the media who'd stabbed Pat in the back—so I was touched to know that, despite everything else he was going through, he was still thinking of his players.

Pat's lessons taught me how to be a better hockey player. He was right about a lot of things. He really was one of a kind, and I was lucky to be able to play for him.

7

The Clown Show

AFTER ALL the success we had under Pat Burns, the next two seasons were not fun. We finished last in our division both years, and a flurry of trades meant that the roster was shaken up several times. It didn't look like we were headed in the right direction and there were few signs of improvement, which meant that we were in need of a big overhaul to turn the team around. It took us two years to get the right group of guys together and start having success. Then, in the summer of 1998, the Leafs hired Pat Quinn to take over as our new head coach.

I am often asked about the differences between Pat Burns and Pat Quinn. Both were special coaches and both had a big impact on my career and my life. The biggest difference between the two was that if you found yourself in Burns's doghouse, there was no getting out of it. Ever. Because when Burnsie made his mind up, he didn't change it, and he hated guys who kissed his ass. But Quinn could be convinced to give a player a second chance.

Which was good, because after our performance as a team the past two seasons, all of us needed a second chance.

Pat Quinn had an immediate impact on the team. He was a winner in his first game as coach of the Leafs when we beat the Red Wings 2–1 at Maple Leaf Gardens. Curtis Joseph made 38 saves that night, while I picked up an assist and fought Darren McCarty. That was the start of a run of success that would carry us through the next six years. Not only did we make the playoffs in Quinn's first season, but we beat the Philadelphia Flyers and Pittsburgh Penguins in the playoffs and made it all the way to the Eastern Conference final against Buffalo.

Quinn believed in the core guys on the team and our ability to calmly and confidently lead the way with our experience. He believed in us because he knew that we had a solid group. And he allowed Mats and me, along with the other veterans, like Cabers—Bryan McCabe—to run the room. Quinn knew that you can sometimes get the best out of people by leaving them alone. He trusted us right from the start—trusted that we would be responsible, that we knew what we had to do, and that we would put the team ahead of ourselves. He would say that just like a carpenter, hockey players have to pay attention to every little detail. He created an atmosphere on his teams where, if you didn't play the right way and you weren't responsible, you weren't going to last.

One time, while I was playing under Quinn, I had an issue with a guy on the team who was talking badly about me behind my back. Things came to a head with an incident in Edmonton. After that trip, Quinn called me into his office and asked me what the problem was. I didn't want to tell him, but Quinn knew something was really bothering me. It turns out that this guy had already been sent down to the minors. That's when I knew I was one of Pat's guys.

Pat knew that there was no letdown in my game. He would go to bat for me because he knew that he could get every ounce out of me. That's a big reason why I played so much more in the playoffs under Quinn than I had on any other team. During the regular season, I would always tease Pat that it was almost like he was saving me for the playoffs. But when we got there, he really believed in me, and my playing time proved it. To me, that was the ultimate compliment, but also the ultimate responsibility. Pat was giving me the time to make a difference, and I made sure I worked for it. Quinn didn't give you respect; you had to earn it. There was no entitlement. I was a true believer in that, and I still am to this day.

I was one of the few players Quinn would joke around with on a regular basis. He liked to make fun of me to keep everybody relaxed. Quinn and I would go at it, back and forth. It was all in good fun, and the guys loved it. Between the two of us, we kept things pretty loose in front of the team. Often, when something unexpected happened in the dressing room with Pat, everybody would look to me to see how I reacted. Usually, I couldn't help but laugh. Bryan McCabe and Mats were the worst—they would look at me, and suddenly the whole room would burst out laughing.

Still, I had to make sure that things never went too far. One of Pat's biggest strengths was making sure that we never got too high and we never got too low. I never forgot that lesson—that in any walk of life, you have to find a balance. A big part of leading a team involves maintaining that balance. If the vibe in the room was too relaxed, guys wouldn't take anything seriously or show the proper respect. But if the team atmosphere was too strict, guys would feel like they couldn't blow off steam and they'd think too much. Pat was a big guy, and he always struggled to bend over and pick up his marker, which he always seemed to drop whenever he wrote on the whiteboard in the dressing room. To save Pat from bending over to grab the marker, someone would have to jump in and pick it up for him—usually, it was one of the assistant coaches, Ricky Ley or Woody (Keith) Acton. Some guys thought this was hilarious, and anytime Pat dropped his marker, they'd glance at me to see what I would do, almost as though they wanted me to laugh so that they would have permission to do the same. But I always refused to react. Even though Pat and I could tease each other, he was still the coach, and guys had to respect his authority. I knew that if I made a face or whispered something to the guy next to me, the entire dressing room would laugh their heads off, and Pat would be pissed. There's a difference between joking around with someone and making them into a joke, and we had to make sure we never took things too far.

But sometimes you can't help but let loose, and luckily we all got along well enough as a team that nobody ever got hurt by it; we just had so much fun. When Pat went to clean the whiteboard, he'd use his hand to wipe it down. Then, while he was talking, he'd wipe his hands together, and at some point, he'd end up touching his face, smearing the marker ink all over it. Here was this big, handsome guy, well dressed in a suit, and he'd have black stripes running all across his face. You couldn't help but laugh.

At Christmastime, I used to call Pat "Frosty." Every year at Christmas, Pat would wear the same Frosty the Snowman tie. The first time we saw it, we couldn't wait for the next winter to come around so we could see it again. Year after year, as we got close to the holidays, Pat would stroll into the dressing room wearing his usual serious face and his Frosty the Snowman tie. The guys knew it was coming, so they'd already have towels in front of their faces, trying to hold it in and not get caught laughing out loud. The problem was that I just couldn't hold it in. Pat would ask me what I was laughing at, and I'd just point at his tie. I only had to look at Bryan McCabe, directly across the room from me, and I'd lose it. My laughter would set the other guys off, and before we knew it, the whole room would be howling. I sometimes think that Quinn knew exactly how we'd react, and that he wore the tie so we could blow off steam laughing like that. It goes to show you how confident he was and how well he could read his team.

In my time with the Leafs, the guys who knew me the best— besides Mats—were Pat Burns and Pat Quinn. They just understood me more than everyone else. But when it comes to the best mentor I ever had in the art of yelling at the refs, it was Quinn, by a long shot. Pat loved to yell at the refs. I always knew the exact moment when Pat really got into the game: it was when he would start to yell at the refs. And he would do it every night, so you knew he was always in the game. I had a much different relationship with the refs and linesmen than Pat did. Ray Scapinello was my favourite on-ice official; I just knew he would be honest and fair. I had a good relationship with most of the referees and linesmen because they all appreciated how tough my job was. Hockey is an emotional game, and the refs know that anyone and everyone can get worked up a bit in the heat of the game. There were always a few young guys among the refs with egos, but most of them came around. But as far as Pat was concerned, there was never a ref he didn't want to yell at.

I played for Pat through his entire ten-year run as the coach of the Leafs. Not only did we win a lot of games during those years, but, as Bryan McCabe once put it to me, we had a "clown show" going on there in Toronto for a while. There isn't a better example of that than the night in Philadelphia in March 2001 when a fan fell into the penalty box with me. His name was Chris Falcone, and the incident set off a number of lawsuits.

First off, you have to remember that fans in Philadelphia are intense. They were awesome, and I used to love playing there, but they would do and say just about anything to you. Anytime you went into Philly to take on the Flyers, you had to be ready for that. Now, I had spent my entire life training myself to be able to react to any situation on the ice at a moment's notice. And that skill sure came in handy that night in Philly. I was sitting in the penalty box, and, as usual, the Flyers fans around the box were really giving me the business. They were hanging over the glass and calling me every name in the book. I grabbed the water bottle sitting next to me and squirted some Gatorade on the fans behind me to cool them off. It wasn't supposed to be an aggressive move, but Falcone didn't like it, and he jumped up against the glass to shout at me. I stood up with my back against the penalty box door to get out of Falcone's reach, and I went to squirt him again with the water bottle. Later, Falcone said that he was trying to grab the water bottle out of my hand. But he was a little front-heavy, and whatever he was trying to do, all of a sudden the glass he was leaning on gave out and Falcone fell face-first towards me into the penalty box. He slid down the glass onto the bench, and we fought briefly until linesman Kevin Collins jumped into the box to break things up. By this point, the arena in Philly was a total gong show. Curtis Joseph later told me it was like watching someone fall into the lion's den at the zoo. The entire arena was chanting, "Domi sucks!" at the top of their lungs as I was pulled out onto the ice. I wasn't upset—to be honest, it all happened so fast, I barely registered what had happened. On the ice, I tried to explain to the rest of the officials what had taken place. They got things sorted out pretty quickly, and security escorted the guy out of the arena as I went back and took my seat in the penalty box.

In an interview after the game, I told reporters that I thought the entire thing had been some sort of early April Fool's joke. I thought that was the end of it, but the circus on the ice only got crazier off of it. Ironically, if you watch the video of the incident, you can hear TV announcer Harry Neale saying to partner Joe Bowen, "Watch the lawsuit, Tie. Watch the lawsuit." How right he was. Falcone did sue me, but I won both court cases brought against me. That could have settled it, but Falcone kept appealing the decision. The legal team I was employing cost a ton of money, so I couldn't understand why or how Falcone kept the legal drama going; it turned out his relative was a lawyer.

So, one day, in 2003, I had a breakfast meeting at the Four Seasons with my three lawyers. This was before the morning skate on the day of a game late in the regular season. We already knew that we would be playing the Flyers in the first round of the playoffs. I met with the lawyers and told them that the joke was over. They were all great guys, but the Leafs weren't paying my legal bills and I couldn't afford to keep defending myself against Falcone. Who knows how much that breakfast alone was costing me? But I also knew that Falcone was a blue-collar guy, and I figured I could relate to him. So I told my lawyers that I wanted Falcone's phone number so that I could call him myself. They advised me against it, but I insisted, and eventually, they gave me his number.

Later that day, on the team bus, I said to Mats that I was going to call this guy. Mats was shocked. "You're going to do what?" he asked. I turned to him and said, "I am going to call him. Watch."

And I gave Falcone a call.

"Hello, Falcone; it's Tie Domi."

Falcone immediately started yelling, demanding to know who was screwing around with him and telling me to stop it right away.

"No, Falcone, it's Tie Domi. Here's my phone number. Call me back—it's me. Please call me back."

I hung up and the phone rang almost instantly.

"I told you, man. So, listen, this is what I want to do. Are you going to the game tonight?" I asked. Falcone said he was.

"Okay, I am going to put your name at security. I want to meet you after the game—just you and me. I'll have security bring you to the room and I just want to talk to you face-to-face."

"Really?" Falcone asked.

"Seriously, man, it would be nice to meet you face-to-face."

And Falcone agreed.

As soon as I got off the ice after the game, he was down there. Ken Dryden, who was the president of the Leafs at the time, tried to join us so that he could monitor what I said or did, but I told him that Falcone and I needed to meet one-on-one; this was a time for street smarts. Ken told me to make sure that the media didn't find out about the meeting. I looked at Ken, wondering if he was joking. Of course I didn't want the media to find out; I didn't need Ken to tell me that.

I walked into the room wearing just the hockey leggings and long underwear that I always had on under my equipment. Falcone looked at me, wondering what the heck I was going to do. I stuck my hand out, grabbed his hand, and hugged him. I said to him, "You're a good guy. I'm a good guy. How many kids do you have?" He told me he had two kids.

"I'll tell you what, I will fly you and your family up to Toronto. I will put you up at the Royal York Hotel, and I will get you tickets— four seats together—for the first two games of the series."

"Yeah?" he asked.

"Yeah," I said.

That handshake agreement was good enough for me, but to make it official, we signed all of the paperwork that I'd brought with me. As I was leaving, I said to Falcone, "Let's not tell the media about this. Don't make a big deal about it." Of course, word got out, and as soon as Falcone got to the game in Toronto, he was doing interviews in the crowd. But I didn't care; he had his moment, and we were able to resolve our differences the old-school way. No hiding behind lawyers or running around—just a face-to-face meeting where a handshake could seal the deal. And at the end of it, everyone that Falcone was trying to sue—me, the Flyers organization, the NHL—got off. Win-win, if you ask me.

* * *

I may not have a lot of formal education, but I do have street smarts. And I pride myself on the fact that I have a lot of common sense. And believe me, those two things can take you a long way. Throughout my playing career and my post-hockey life, they have allowed me to stand up to guys who, on paper, were a lot smarter than me. Ken Dryden is one of those guys. Ken has plenty of degrees, and he's trained as a lawyer, but book smarts and street smarts aren't always the same thing. One incident I had with Ken when he was the president of the Leafs only reinforced how important having common sense can be.

I will never forget walking into the Air Canada Centre for the morning skate of what was our very first game at the new rink. This would have been February 20, 1999. We were playing the Montreal Canadiens that night, so, as you could imagine, it was going to be a big event.

When I arrived for the morning skate, I walked into the dressing room, where I was surprised to see a letter posted on the whiteboard, advising that the players would have to park across the street that night, instead of under the new arena that had just been built with a big underground parking garage. It was a weird instruction, so I asked the trainers who was responsible for the letter. Turns out it was Ken Dryden who posted it.

I had to head out for the morning skate, but I asked the trainers to ask Dryden down to Pat's office so that I could speak with him afterwards. When I got on the ice for practice, I told Pat I'd called a meeting in his office. Pat laughed as I told him I'd do all the talking. After I'd taken off my gear and showered, I made my way to Pat's office. I was the last guy to walk into the room, and I found Dryden, Mats, and Pat sitting there. Ken didn't seem happy; he wouldn't even look at me. I made eye contact with Mats and Pat and made a face as if to say, "Is this guy serious?"

"Is there a problem about parking across the street?" he asked. "Do you have an issue with that?"

"I'm not parking across the street," I replied. "I'm parking underground, and so is everybody else. It's opening night of a new building—it's going to be crazy out there tonight, so if you think I'm going to walk across the street with my kids through all the fans, you're out of your mind."

Ken started to talk about "engaging" with the fans and having to do this and that. He said, "You have to *integrate* with the people, and they have to touch and feel the players." Then he started talking about how I had to imagine "that one little boy you sign that autograph for." That's when I lost it.

I loved the Montreal Canadiens as a kid. Guy Lafleur was one of my all-time favourites. I knew and respected a lot of those guys whom I'd idolized as a kid, and I knew how much their signature could mean to a young fan. But the crowds in the early days of Lafleur's career were a lot different than they were when I was playing. So I simply said, "I'm parking underground and so are my teammates." I walked out, and that night, everybody parked underground for the first game at the Air Canada Centre.

Common sense is what leadership is all about. Leaders need to recognize that sometimes the best ideas don't work in the real world. In that situation with Ken Dryden, my instincts told me that having to get through a crowd of fans at a new arena would be a terrible idea—especially as a lot of us had young kids—and I felt like I had to speak up for what I thought was right. Good leaders listen when someone comes to them with something to say.

* * *

During those years under Pat Quinn, a lot of team problems were solved in the laundry room, away from any reporters. At the ACC, the laundry room was at the rear of the dressing room. We referred to it as "the office." That was the real office, where things got done and issues were resolved privately. Through much of the ten years Mats and I were together, Pat relied on us to run the room. A lot of guys came and went, but the two of us had a good grip on things.

Between us, we could usually find a solution to any problem by ourselves.

That was the thing about my time with the Leafs—even in the years when we had average teams, we still found a way to win games and get into the playoffs. It helped that we had some fundamentals, like good goaltending and great leadership, but it was also because we had a lot of guys on the team that I called warriors. To me, a warrior was a guy who would do anything to win and who always had your back. Warriors are the real winners and leaders, and they are the guys who play hard every shift. Guys like Gary Roberts immediately come to mind. When you are that way yourself, it's easy to identify those sorts of guys on a team.

But those years with Pat Quinn weren't always good. There were some rough times that I had to deal with as well. The infamous Scott Niedermayer incident is the one that stands out as probably the darkest mark on my career.

After sweeping the Ottawa Senators in four straight games in the opening round of the 2001 playoffs, we knew we were in for a real battle with our next opponent, the New Jersey Devils. The Devils were the defending Stanley Cup champions, and they looked ready to make another deep run in the postseason. Curtis Joseph was amazing in Game 1 as we opened the series with a big-time 2–0 win in New Jersey. Game 2 of the series was also in New Jersey, and we ended up losing 6–5 in overtime. During that game, I chirped Devils defenceman Scott Niedermayer. I was trying to get into his head, so I went to the end of our bench and yelled over the glass separating us from the Devils' bench: "I'm going to run you. Every shift, I'm dumping it in your corner."

He responded, "You're going to have to go through my Easton," referring to his stick.

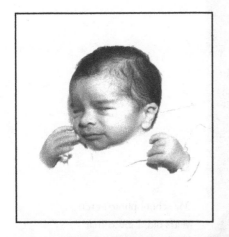

Me in the hospital in 1969. Like I said, I've always had a big head.

My mom, Meyrem; my sister, Trish; my brother, Dash; my dad, John; and me.

My school photo at ten years old. I loved that *Starsky & Hutch* shirt.

My first hockey team. I could barely skate, so my dad, John, had to sponsor the team's jerseys just to get me on the team.

The 1979–80 Belle River Silver Stick Champions.

Eleven years old with the 1981 Chatham Moose Lodge team of the Chatham Minor Hockey Association.

In 1983, at thirteen years old, soccer was still my best sport.

Corey Foster and Dan Jensen were two of my close friends
when I played on the Petes at eighteen years old.

My dad and brother were by my side at the Montreal Forum when
I was selected 27th overall by the Toronto Maple Leafs at the NHL
Entry Draft on June 11, 1988.

On my way to picking up
37 penalty minutes in my
first NHL game on
March 2, 1990.

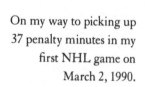

© GRAIG ABEL/GRAIG ABEL PHOTOGRAPHY

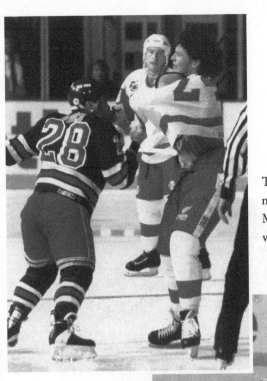

Taking on the king and my celebration right after. Madison Square Garden was electric that night.

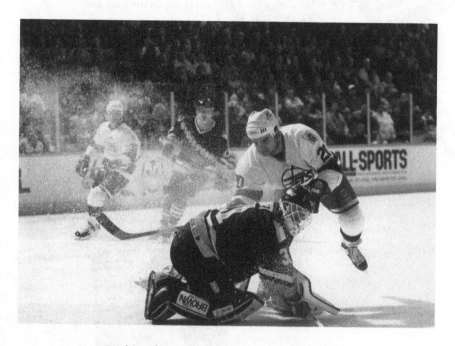

Crashing the net against the Pittsburgh Penguins.

(*Left to right*) Dave Ellett, me, Nick Kypreos, Wendel Clark, and Adam Graves.

Dancing with my mom at my wedding in Toronto in 1993.

From friend to family member, Adam Graves is one of the most genuine and kindest people I have ever met.

Between a hockey career and being a new dad, I could always use some rest in those early days. Luckily, my kids always had smiles on their faces.

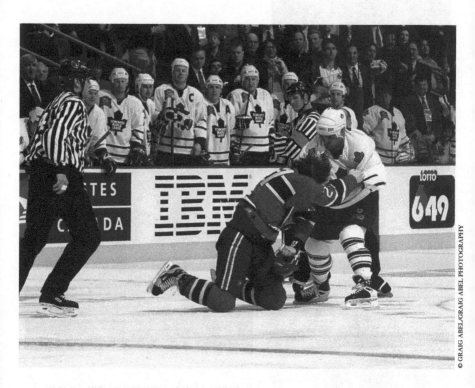

© GRAIG ABEL/GRAIG ABEL PHOTOGRAPHY

At times like this, with everyone's eyes on me, I knew I had to do
whatever it took to stand up for my teammates.

Rob Ray and I were big rivals with a lot of respect for each other.

In 1996 and 1997, I traded my skates for cleats and played as the Toronto Argonauts kicker in a couple of preseason games to raise money for Sick Kids Hospital. Playing with athletes like Doug Flutie helped me enjoy every day of my career.

It helped that I never forgot where I came from. In 2006, the Albanian Embassy presented me with the same distinction awarded to Mother Teresa and John Belushi.

Side by side with Mats, ready to react to whatever the job demanded and help lead us wherever we needed to go.

© GRAIG ABEL/GRAIG ABEL PHOTOGRAPHY

Everything that I've learned and accomplished has always been done with one thing in mind: making the best life possible for my family. Carlin, Max, and Avery—and now my nephew, Devan—are the best part of my life, and I couldn't be prouder of them.

I decided right then and there that I was going to run Niedermayer all series long. Every chance I got, I would dump the puck into Niedermayer's corner so that I had an opportunity to go after him.

Later that game, I decided to follow up on my talk. Niedermayer went to play the puck along the boards, and I lined him up. Just as I came in to deliver the hit, he lifted his stick to the side while looking the other way, shoving his stick right in my face as I was moving full speed. The stick sliced me wide open between my upper lip and my nose. Sometimes that's an accident, and it's something you have to be prepared for in hockey. But I didn't see this as an accident. At the start of the next period, I stood at centre ice between the benches, and I picked Niedermayer out on the Devils' bench. He had an "I told you so" look on his face, so, with blood dripping down my face, I calmly said to him, "I might not get you tonight. But I will get you."

The series moved back to Toronto for Game 3, and once again we lost in overtime, this time by a score of 3–2. Every game of the series was proving to be high intensity and full of emotion, and it was a close battle the whole way. On May 3, we were back at the Air Canada Centre for Game 4. The arena was really rocking that night. We were down 2–1 in the series, and everyone knew we desperately needed a win if we were going to have a chance to win it. And we were pulling it off. We played a tight game and we had a 3–1 lead with only a few minutes left to play. In fact, I was having the best game of my career. I already had an assist and had logged over fifteen minutes of ice time. Near the end of the third period, the whole building was chanting my name, so Pat Quinn sent me out for a late shift. Don Cherry and Ron MacLean were waiting for me in the TV studio because I was going to be the first star of the game. It looked like I was going to be able to mark this down as one of the most memorable games in my career.

I saw Niedermayer chasing the puck into our end. I knew his route—he liked to skate down the wing and then curl back up along the boards. He was an incredible skater, and he had the speed to get back to his end before most other skaters got there.

There were twenty-three seconds left in the game when I jumped over the boards. I wasn't thinking of people chanting my name or that we were winning the game. I was only thinking of Niedermayer and how I wanted to get back at him.

Then, with seven seconds left in the game, I hit him. I honestly thought I was just going to give him a shot to rattle him and that would be it. I never intended to injure him or hit him square in the head and knock him out cold. I threw out my left elbow—I wanted to remind him that I hadn't forgotten what his stick had done to me. With my luck, I ended up nailing him right on the button. Not many people—not even the referees—saw the hit. Devils defenceman Scott Stevens did, though. He was in the penalty box at the time, and he was livid. I wish Stevens had been on the ice. I chased him my whole career, but he would never fight me. Seven seconds before I would have been in the dressing room celebrating a playoff win, and I had just gone and made what was far and away the stupidest decision of my career.

As they were loading Niedermayer on the stretcher, I stood by Curtis Joseph and said, "CuJo, I'm done." After the game, Pat said, "I knew I shouldn't have put you on the ice. But you didn't have to hit him on the button." Later in the series, I went to find Niedermayer so that I could apologize to him in person. I found him in the hallway outside his dressing room, but he didn't want to shake my hand. I didn't blame him—I can only imagine how angry he was.

I apologized to my teammates for what happened. They knew

I felt horrible about it. They tried to make me feel better by saying things like, "Hey, stuff happens in hockey." But Niedermayer's injury didn't just happen; I had caused it, and by doing so, I had gone against every value I had promised I would hold myself to. I knew I was going to be suspended and that the league would throw the book at me. And I was right: the NHL suspended me for the remainder of the playoffs and the first eight games of the following season.

If there is one moment from my NHL career I wish I could take back or change, it would be that one. If I hadn't hit Niedermayer, I wouldn't have been suspended, and I know I could have made a difference over the rest of the series. I wouldn't have given ammunition to the people who already preached against fighting in the game. But I did do it, and I accept the responsibility for my actions. Hitting Niedermayer like that was the dumbest thing I did in my career. That's no excuse, but I have never said that I was perfect and, like everything else that's happened to me in my life, I've lived with and learned from that moment every day since. I learn from my mistakes, just like everyone else.

* * *

We had an amazing run under Quinn for a number of reasons, but a major factor was our goaltending. Quinn was hired as coach of the Leafs at the same time that management signed Curtis Joseph to be our new starting goalie. There's an old saying in the NHL: "Show me a good goalie and I'll show you a good coach." Pat was a very good coach, but there's no question that CuJo was incredible for us most nights, and he was a big reason why we went to the conference finals in 1999 and 2002.

When CuJo left, he was replaced by Eddie Belfour. Eddie was different, but he was also an excellent goalie—he's in the Hall of Fame for a reason. Eddie was outstanding, and he led us to the playoffs his first two years with the Leafs. In fact, during those two seasons in Toronto, Eddie had 17 shutouts. He was an interesting guy, and I always liked and respected him. That being said, I will never forget what happened one night in Calgary.

It was March 11, 2003, and we had just picked up Doug Gilmour at the trade deadline. We were in Calgary at the time, and the team had a few days off, so we all went out one night. Eddie and Robert Svehla—two great teammates—started drinking Crown Royal shots. If you want to just put a match to gasoline to start a fire, that's the way to do it. The place started getting busy, and before it was even ten o'clock, Matt Stajan and some of the young guys on the team came over to Mats and me. "Guys, you better go see Eddie," Stajan said.

I looked at Mats and said, "You're the captain. Go take care of it."

Mats responded, "*You* go." I tracked Eddie down and found him challenging anyone who would listen to arm-wrestling contests. Because Eddie was a legend even then, there were plenty of fans who wanted to arm wrestle him. Unfortunately, Eddie's also really intense, and he hates losing. After he lost one match too many, he demanded a rematch, and then, when the guy refused, Eddie wanted to fight him. That wasn't going to happen, so I grabbed Nik Antropov, Alex Ponikarovsky, and Dave "Stone Cold" Griffiths, and all four of us escorted Eddie out of the bar and got him into a cab with me sitting on his feet, Nik sitting on his head, and Poni holding him in the middle. It took all three of us to hold Eddie down in the back of the cab.

When we got back to the hotel, we had to force Eddie through the lobby. We were staying at the Palliser Hotel, and as we were manhandling Eddie to the elevator, there were families checking in at the front desk who had come into town for the weekend to watch us play. They couldn't believe what they were seeing. Every time the elevator door went to close, Eddie would stick his foot out to block it. He was determined to get back to the bar and win one last arm-wrestling contest. When we finally got Eddie to the room, he kept trying to escape. It wasn't like Eddie to act this way. But finally, I figured enough was enough, so I said, "Eddie, you know that I love you." And with that, I punched Eddie in the face and knocked him out cold. He was fast asleep the rest of the night.

Eddie had accidentally ripped up my clothes as we wrestled him back to his room, and I was sweaty from the workout it took to get him in there, so I ended up having to take a shower and change my clothes before rejoining the team. It was at least an hour before I returned to the bar, and when I got there, Mats asked, "Where have you been? Where did you go?"

"Shut the hell up," I told him. "I'll tell you tomorrow."

The next day, the first thing I did was call our trainer, Scott McKay, and say, "I think I killed the Beagle," using my nickname for Eddie. Scott promised to go check in on Eddie, so I made my way down to the hotel restaurant to wait to see how Eddie was doing. Mats and I had breakfast together, and as we sat there, I told him everything. When I finished, all he could say was, "No. Way."

"Yeah," I replied. "I really hit the Beagle hard. I feel bad."

As soon as I said that, out of the corner of my eye, I saw Eddie come walking into the restaurant. He was moving really slowly, and his eye was swollen. He came over to me, and I got ready to apologize. As I looked up at him, he gave me a hug, and before I could say anything, he said, "Tie, thanks, man." And that was it—the incident was over, and it was time to move on.

* * *

Of all the teammates I played with during my time with the Leafs, one of my all-time favourites was Wade Belak. Belak arrived in Toronto in February 2001, when the Leafs claimed him off waivers from the Calgary Flames. Wade and I would be teammates until the end of my career.

When he came to Toronto, Wade was a tough kid, but he was losing fights. He came to me and asked me to work with him, and I agreed, of course. I showed him what I knew and tried to teach him some of the tricks of the trade that had served me well over my NHL career. Pretty soon, Wade and I were roommates on the road and were sitting next to each other in the dressing room. Wade ended up sitting next to me for five years. I groomed him and taught him how to do the job we were given and how to be a good teammate. But more than anything, I always tried to keep him involved with whatever the team was doing. I didn't care how much he played, which wasn't much, and whether or not he was a healthy scratch now and then; I did everything I could to make him one of the lead voices in the dressing room. Wade was a great guy to have around, and with his friendly nature and sense of humour, he could have anybody and everybody in the dressing room laughing. This guy, every day that he sat next to you, he brightened up your life. I wanted others to see the potential that I saw in him. To help with that, I made Wade the new fine-master for the team.

It's known now, but during Wade's time in Toronto, not many people were aware that he struggled with depression. I didn't know the full extent of Wade's difficulties, but I could see when he was going through a down period. In a lot of ways, I could relate to Wade, and we were close, so I could tell when he didn't feel right or when a dark mood was setting in. Wade really didn't like fighting, so on the nights when he was likely going to fight someone, he wasn't the same person. At times like that, I had to keep him calm. I would do my best to support him, cheer him up, and just listen to whatever he had to say.

For a full year after I stepped away from the game, I didn't go back to the Air Canada Centre at all. I had no desire to. I just wanted to back off and let the other guys have their time. I'd had my time there, and now it was their turn. The first time I went back was in 2007. Wade's wife, Jenn, had asked me to stop by the rink and talk to Wade. She told me he had been feeling really down, and she felt that he needed to talk to someone he could trust. After the first intermission, once the team had gone back out on the ice, I went down to the dressing room. When I got there, I found Wade sitting alone in the weight room with his head in his hands.

"Beeler," I said.

He lifted his head. "Hey, Tie," he replied quietly.

He just wasn't the same person. Since I had left, something had changed; you could tell something wasn't right with him. He had been a healthy scratch for a long time—almost twenty games at that point. I think that, after I'd left, nobody knew how to handle him. All Wade ever wanted was to feel a part of the team. He never asked for much, but when you sit out for as long as he did, it can get to you.

Wade and I talked a long time that night, and I hoped he would see a break in the days following that. But just the opposite happened. In March of that year, Tomas Kaberle took a cheap shot from Cam Janssen of the Devils. The next time the Leafs went to play New Jersey, Wade, of course, was put in the lineup so that he could respond to what happened. I could see it coming—it's the same sort of thing I had to do when I played. Wade did his job. He went out that game and fought Janssen. The next game, Wade was out of the lineup again as a healthy scratch. That was it. He didn't dress for another game the rest of the season. It was hard for Wade, never knowing what night he might be told to fight, only to be passed over the next game once he'd done what was needed of him. Over the final four years of his NHL career, Wade only played in 124 out of a possible 328 games.

Athletes are human beings. Entertainers are human beings. Everybody has issues, no matter what you do in life. I later learned that Wade had mental health issues. I had tried to do the best I could to cheer him up and make him feel like he was needed. But I didn't know how bad things really were until after I retired. I only knew the positive, happy, and loving version of Wade because that's what we brought out in him every day.

While I learned that Wade had depression, I never in a million years thought he would die so young—certainly not just five years after we played together. The news of Wade's death in August 2011 was devastating to hear. I got the news while I was driving Max to London, Ontario, for his first training camp. I got a phone call telling me that one of my ex-teammates had been found dead in a hotel room. I asked who it was—it was Wade. I broke the news to Max and we both started crying.

What I witnessed at Wade's funeral was just as difficult. It summed up my career for me. The life of an enforcer is thankless.

The pressures are constant, and others always come first. You have one job to do, and it's not very glamorous. If you're going to make a career out of it, you have to be willing to do your job without expecting to be showered with praise. But even given all that, you never want your teammates to feel sorry for you or feel like they owe you. Wade Belak fought for a lot of guys in Toronto. So I was shocked when I flew down to Wade's funeral in Nashville, Tennessee, and discovered that, of his Leaf teammates, only Bryan McCabe, trainer Scott McKay, and I were there.

That funeral really woke me up. I was disgusted. Daymond Langkow was supposed to speak, but he couldn't bring himself to do it. Just before the ceremony started, he came up to me and said, "Tie, none of us can do this. Can you speak for us?" I looked at Bryan and said, "Caber, you're coming with me." Wade's wife and two daughters were sitting in the front row, right in front of the podium. Seeing those two young kids there and knowing that they wouldn't have their father in their life anymore, I felt like I owed it to them to hold it together. You only get to say goodbye once. Bryan and I managed to do the whole eulogy together, speaking from the heart about Wade and our time with him.

I travelled back to Toronto right after the funeral. It was a long day, but I was still able to fly home, shower, and change before heading to a former teammate's engagement party that night— it had been planned before we found out about Wade's funeral. When I got to the party, I saw a lot of guys we had all played with on the Leafs, and I was really disappointed. Wade had been the ultimate teammate, and none of those guys had managed to attend his funeral. They could have hopped on a plane, gone to the funeral, and been home, all in a day. It isn't as though they didn't have the money to do it. But they just couldn't get it; they didn't understand why that was so important. When you see a guy who battles for the other guys on his team, you expect a lot of his ex-teammates to come and pay their respects. The fact that Wade didn't have that really bothered me that night, and it still does. It was a clear reminder that what we do in the NHL isn't our life; it's just our livelihood.

Wade's death made me reflect on my own career and my time in the NHL. I became a well-known name and face in Canada for being a hockey player. I was able to live and provide a good life for my family and meet a lot of interesting people because of it. But hockey was never my whole life; it was always just a part of it. I loved Wade Belak from the first time I met him, because I knew right away that he was a good guy. In Wade, you saw a guy who knew how to have fun, a guy who made you happy to be around him. And then, suddenly, he was gone. But everybody kept living their lives, and the day-to-day routines went on. I now wonder, if I were gone tomorrow, who would show up to say goodbye to me? After Wade's funeral, I wouldn't be surprised if only a few showed up. Nobody owes me anything. I have a clear conscience about my actions, and I work hard to always have a positive attitude. I focus on what I can control, have an impact on people while I still can, and surround myself with people I care about. When you're gone, you're gone, so why not enjoy the ride? And while you're enjoying life, why not treat people the right way as you go?

Since I retired from the NHL, I've learned to take life one day at a time. I feel grateful for everything that I have in life because I have lost some real close friends over the years—Bob Probert, Wade Belak, Pat Burns, Pat Quinn. And I didn't just lose people in my professional life. A very special friend I'd known since I was eighteen years old, Gary Zentil, passed away not that long ago. He was one of the sweetest people you could have known. He was healthy, and he was one of those guys I could call anytime if I needed to—until suddenly, I couldn't anymore. These are guys who made huge impacts on my life and on my career. Each and every one of them has a special place in my heart.

When people talk about Wade's death, they often talk about fighting and violence in hockey. The more that people try to dissect or demonize fighting in the game, the more I want to make my message positive. People need to remember that not everyone who fought in the NHL ended up with addiction or mental health problems or died young. A lot of guys who were fighters retired from the NHL and have gone on with their lives without any lingering problems. They may just be lucky, or they may have played the game at a time when it was easier to have that kind of role. I don't have an answer; I am not one of those people who can weigh in on concussions and the other health issues that some guys in hockey today are going through. To me, fighting was never about the thrill or the blood or anything like that. It was a job—a demanding one—that could wear people down under the wrong circumstances. It was even harder being the guy that everyone wanted to beat. But no two people are the same, and I recognize that what helped me get through all of that might not be possible for other people.

I have always believed that life is too short to be negative. Moments like Wade's death and his funeral—and more important, the memory of his life—are another reminder to set your sights high and to never be afraid to ask for help to get there. More than anything, Wade's life is a lesson that we should live every day to the fullest.

8

What It Takes to Win

MAKING THE playoffs is tough. Winning multiple rounds is even tougher. I was lucky enough to play on some good teams in my career, and to be a part of a lot of good playoff runs. That's what I miss most. Thanks to Pat Quinn's trust in me, I ended up playing more playoff games for the Leafs than Darryl Sittler, Doug Gilmour, Mats Sundin, and Wendel Clark. I didn't win a Cup, but I did play the second-most playoff games of all right-wingers in Leaf history, behind only George Armstrong.

For me, playoff hockey was vastly different from the regular season. During the regular season, in every game of my career, I had to be ready to react to whatever situation might arise, whether it was fighting an opponent who had done something to one of my teammates or, when things weren't going our way, getting into a fight to change the momentum of the game. In the playoffs, fighting was less of a concern. Teams were focused on winning, and that meant they wanted their tough guys out making a difference on the ice, not sitting in the penalty box. To do that, teams needed guys who could skate and who had a hockey IQ. A hockey IQ and a classroom IQ are very different things, but the former all boils down to common sense and good judgment. When I had an assignment, I knew what I had to do. I wasn't one for school, but I did have the skills and mind-set to play a checking role, so in the playoffs, I became more of a checker than a fighter.

I had my greatest success in the postseason in my years with the Leafs. Of the 86 playoff games I played during my Maple Leafs career, 24 of them came against one of our biggest rivals, the Ottawa Senators. We faced the Senators in the postseason four times over a five-year span. And it still makes me proud to say that we won every one of those series. Some people during that time liked to call those Leafs teams the "Bay Street Bullies," harking back to the Broad Street Bullies in Philadelphia in the 1970s. None of us really liked the name, especially Mats—he was no bully. But we cared about winning and moving on to the next round in the playoffs. So if we had to push around a few teams along the way to get there, then so be it. Years after I retired, I was in a pub in New York on American Thanksgiving when a woman approached me. It turned out she was from Ottawa, and she was curious about our playoff rivalry with the Sens. She asked me how it felt to be in Ottawa during road games and to hear all of the opposing fans chanting, "Domi sucks!" She was surprised when I told her that I loved it. I said that if I could, I would actually thank all the fans in Ottawa, as well as the ones in the other twenty-nine arenas across the NHL. Their chants let me know that I was doing my job; all that hate directed towards me kept me in the game and on my toes. It was fun! The fans' insults never bothered me; they only made me more determined to do my job, win the game, and shut them up. Other players might have been bothered by an arena full of fans telling them they sucked, but that kind of garbage only excited me.

There were lots of reasons for our playoff success against Ottawa. Each season, we were backstopped by an outstanding goalie, we had skilled players, we were led by a great coach, and we proved to be the tougher team. Add that all up, and we had a recipe for success. And in each series, we had one player who stepped up and came through at a clutch moment. In 2000, it was Steve "Stumpy" Thomas with two points in the series-clinching game. In 2001, Yanic Perreault scored two goals in the final game of the series. In 2002, Alexander Mogilny's skill helped us outlast the Sens over seven games, and in 2004, Bryan McCabe led the way with a goal and an assist in the final game of the series.

But one thing stayed the same year after year: the entire team showed a willingness to do anything and everything needed to win. Pure skill alone doesn't get it done in the playoffs. There has to be something else deep down inside you that makes you want it more than the other guy. Nowadays, with all the technology and social media out there, there's a lot more emphasis on each individual; there's less of a focus on being part of a team, first and foremost. There are some young players who think that winning just happens. Winning games, especially in the playoffs, doesn't just happen. Nothing just happens. It takes a total commitment from everyone in the lineup, top to bottom, and it doesn't matter who scores as long as you win.

That sort of determination was never clearer than in 2002, when we played the New York Islanders in the first round. It was a vicious seven-game series—so vicious, it was as if there were no puck on the ice. We were just trying to hurt them—I was *definitely* trying to hurt people—and they were trying to hurt us.

Gary Roberts was huge for us in that series. Mats was injured, and Robs was like RoboCop for the whole series. When Robs was in a zone like that, the guy on the other team was either getting out of the way or going through the boards. We all had a will to win, and we made guys on the Islanders accountable. That's why we were able to finally win that crazy series in seven games. We and the Islanders each won all of our home games. Lucky for us, we had home-ice advantage, which made the difference.

That's what made our Leafs team so special in the playoffs: we all knew what it took to win, and we had a dressing room full of warriors who were willing to do whatever that was. Good teams always have good leaders in the dressing room, and we had some amazing ones. Mats was better at that than anyone I knew. He knew how to lead by example, and from the moment he got to the rink until the moment he stepped off the ice, his confidence and determination were clear. We would have followed him anywhere, and he never let us down.

With so much on the line, the playoffs were always an emotional time. They brought out the best or the worst in people as everyone did whatever they could to gain an edge. In 2002, we could feel our series against the Sens slipping out of our hands. We had fallen behind three games to two, and the Sens took a quick 2–0 lead in the first period of Game 6. We were in trouble and someone needed to step up and turn things around in a hurry if we were going to keep our season alive.

The game went back and forth as we traded goals with the Sens. At one point, I went to play the puck on the boards, when, out of the corner of my eye, I could see Ricard Persson coming for me. I knew I had a choice to make. I could play the puck quickly and hope to get out of Persson's way, or I could take the hit and try to use it to my advantage. I have always prided myself on never being one to fake things. But I remembered that the ledge along the old school–style boards in Ottawa was really sharp. So I thought to myself, "What can I do?" and I delayed along the boards, waiting for the hit to land.

I was standing still, a foot away from the boards. Persson had some good speed and slammed into me from behind. It wasn't all that hard of a check, and I figured that Persson would likely get a minor penalty for hitting me from behind. But I knew that if I was bleeding after the hit, he'd be guaranteed a five-minute major penalty. That would mean that, even if we scored, he'd stay in the box; a normal minor penalty would end if we scored a goal. So as I went down, I controlled my fall and turned my head into the boards, head-butting myself off the corner of them. I knew full well that I would get cut wide open. As crazy as it sounds, I collided with the top of the dasher boards to give myself a better chance of getting cut. And it worked. I drew blood—a lot of blood, in fact—on the play, and the refs had an easy call to make on Persson: an automatic five-minute major. That was the beginning of the end for Ottawa that series. They collapsed as we scored two goals on the ensuing power play, went on to win the game 4–3, and forced Game 7.

Although Persson's hit was the most memorable point of that series, it wasn't the hardest check that I had to withstand. Those came from Zdeno Chara. I loved battling Chara. While I respected him, I was constantly harassing him in the playoffs. That wasn't an easy thing to do, given the size difference between us. Chara had nearly a foot on me—he stands six foot nine *without* skates—and I literally had to look up at him or I would be staring at the logo on his jersey. But that didn't stop me from hurtling full speed into his corner every time the puck was there. Chara is a class act, which I respect. Even though he was a young player at the time, he knew his place in the league, and he knew that in the playoffs you do whatever it takes to win. We could always shake each other's hand at the end of a series with a clear conscience. At the end of one series, he said to me, "Oh man, I don't know how you did it. But you're tough; you are a tough player." There is no question that Zdeno Chara is the kind of guy I would want on my team, and I'm not surprised by the success he's had in his career since, with a Stanley Cup win, multiple All-Star nominations, and a Norris Trophy as best defenceman in the NHL.

Our final playoff series against the Senators in 2004 took a real toll on me physically. We were able to beat the Sens in seven games that year, but in Game 4 of the series, I had a scrap with Chris Neil that left me the worse for wear. During the fight, I landed a punch square on the side of Neil's helmet, and the impact broke my left hand. Usually an injury like that would take a guy out of the lineup, but these were the playoffs and I wasn't going to sit out, so I had to find a way to get ready to play as many games as needed.

The problem was that I didn't like the solution the doctors and trainers came up with. If I was to play for the rest of the playoffs, I would have to freeze, so to speak, my hand with injections before every game and in between periods to numb the pain, which would let me use my hand as normally as possible. The issue with that is that I hate needles. No, I *despise* needles. I never liked visiting the doctor or the dentist because I was afraid of having to get a shot, and I really didn't like the sight of blood. I passed out during the birth of two of my three kids! Medicine in general just turned me off. Every time the team doctors wanted me to go on antibiotics, I wouldn't do it. They would tell me that I had to take the pills for seven days, and I just never did. But to make sure I could stay in the lineup for the rest of the playoffs that year, freezing my hand was my only choice. So I agreed to get the shots. I would howl and scream every time the doctors gave me one. The team thought it was hilarious. Every time I went into the trainers' room, Bryan Mc-Cabe would yell out to the rest of the dressing room, "Tie's having another baby!"

My hand was busted so badly, I couldn't practice at all. I couldn't even tie my skates—it was all I could do to be ready for the games. One of the Leafs' trainers, Scott McKay, had to tie my skates for me before every game. He was the best at it because he was the only one who could tie my skates as tight as I like them. So for the remainder of our series with the Sens that year, and for the rest of the 2004 playoffs—including our six-game series with the Flyers—it was like I was a kid again, with Scotty helping me tie my skates so that I could save my hands for the game.

After our 2004 playoff run ended, the doctors told me I should have surgery on my broken hand to repair it. I knew the surgery was necessary, but the timing was terrible. All through the season, the NHL Players' Association and the league executives had been negotiating a new agreement, and there were rumours that there would be a lockout the next season. According to one of the fine-print rules at the time, any player who was on the injured-reserve list couldn't be locked out. That meant they would continue to be paid, even if there was no season. I realized that if I were to follow the doctors' orders and have the surgery they were prescribing, I would be on the injured-reserve list and I would get paid during the lockout. I couldn't stomach that. I didn't want to be one of the guys who got a paycheque while everyone else was locked out. So I bit the bullet and delayed the surgery.

I did whatever it took to get ready to play, no matter how much

I hated it. And I recognized that I wasn't the only one who did that. Lot of guys played through injuries—Mats once played a series with a displaced fracture in his arm. That's just the kind of team we had. No matter how challenging a thing might be, we faced it head-on. We weren't trying to fool anyone or do things the easy way. We just went after the other team nonstop, and we were fully prepared to do whatever it would take to win every battle for a puck, every shift, every game, and every series. Beating a team in a seven-game series isn't easy; doing it year after year is even harder. We all had a part to play, and whether it meant playing through pain, getting my hand frozen with a needle, or allowing someone to slam me headfirst into the boards, I'd do it. Because in the play-offs, you do whatever it takes to win. It's worth it.

9

Behind the Scenes

F ROM THE moment I entered the pro ranks, I enjoyed every day of my NHL career. When I played, I gave it my all on every shift and was determined to leave it all on the ice every night. But I knew my time in the NHL wouldn't last forever, so at the same time that I was focusing on what happened on the ice, I made sure to appreciate my time off of it, too.

When most people hear me say that I had fun during my NHL career, they automatically assume I did a lot of drinking and partying. It surprises a lot of people to hear it, but I wasn't that big of a party guy. Quite honestly, I never even liked the taste of beer. I do like good red wine, but I never have been a big drinker; it just isn't my thing. Too often, I saw others use their stress as an excuse to drink. The funny thing is that, if you could imagine anyone drinking to cope with stress, it would be me. But I never felt like I wanted or needed to drink to get over my job. The only thing I worried about in the NHL was losing my job, but other than that, I had no fear throughout my career. Fear tends to create stress, and that stress can get to people. I was fortunate enough never to have to deal with that problem. Maybe I wasn't scared because I knew there was nobody in the NHL who could hurt me; I just didn't experience pain the same way other people did. Besides not needing the escape from pain or pressure that some people seemed to find in booze or pills, I never wanted to lose control; I had to be sharp.

Although I was never much of a drinker, I always went out with the team and I always had fun. When I was out with the guys, we'd get to the bar and I'd shout, "Let's do some shots!" While everyone was distracted, I would quietly give the bartender a tip and tell them to give me shots of water instead of the vodka they were serving everyone else.

One night, though, my teammates finally caught on to my ruse. It was an end-of-the-year team party in Toronto, and I was sitting with the Russian players on the team—Dmitri Yushkevich, Igor Korolev, Alexander Karpovtsev, and Danny Markov. I knew how to sing songs and swear in Russian, so we liked to hang out together. I had vodka shots for everyone lined up, and I had the group doing one shot every minute. But while the Russians were pounding back the drinks, my shots were just water. The Russians had had at least seven or eight drinks before they caught on to me. It was Markov who called me out. He started yelling in Russian, and suddenly all of the other guys in the group were going on in Russian about how I hadn't done the shots. I still wouldn't do the shots, though—what were they going to do, beat me up?

Whether we were out after a game or getting ready for it in the dressing room, part of my job was to keep the guys relaxed. And I don't think there was anybody else in the NHL who would even think to do what I did to get the boys ready to play. I was one of the first players to wear the skintight long underwear under my equipment that you see so many players wearing now. At first guys laughed at me, but eventually they all started using it. Sometimes, just before I put on my equipment, I'd throw a song on the stereo to get the guys' attention. I'd introduce myself: "Ladies and gentlemen, please welcome to the stage, the lovely and talented . . ." and then I'd pick one guy's wife's or girlfriend's name, and I'd tiptoe out. I'd grab a hockey stick and I'd launch into my version of a striptease dance, using the stick as a pole in the middle of the dressing room. Guys couldn't hold it together. Camaraderie was the key to a good team, and if that meant dancing around the dressing room like a stripper, then I was all for it.

I was also in charge of what I considered to be an important part of the dressing room etiquette: manscaping. I was (and still am) a dedicated manscaper—I'm talking about shaving the chest and all that. I started back when I was in junior, out of necessity. I had to shave everything—I hated hair. I wish I could put all the hair I shaved off my body on the top of my head, where I really need it. When I started manscaping in junior, I'd call out, "Time to get out the Weedwhacker, boys!" and guys would look at me like I was from another planet. But it wasn't long before everybody took it up, and soon we all looked like a bunch of plucked chickens. Somehow we thought it was a good idea at the time. When I got to the NHL, I brought the idea of manscaping, especially to the Europeans. Most of them who came over didn't have a clue about grooming. Tomas Kaberle had one eyebrow when he arrived at Leafs camp. I took one look at him and said, "Kabby, you've got to do something about that unibrow there." Believe it or not, I'm not embarrassed to say I'm even a big manicure and pedicure guy, too.

That was all fun and games, but paying for a meal when you were out with a bunch of teammates was serious business. If you play in the NHL, you quickly learn how to play the credit card game. On nights before a day off, a group of us would often go out to a nice restaurant for a big meal. When it came time to pay the bill, everybody at the table would have to toss his credit card in a napkin. We'd pick cards out one at a time, and whoever's card was picked last would have to pay for the entire meal—for everyone. We're talking thousands of dollars. As Bryan McCabe put it one night when some other guy had to pay, "Free food always tastes better, doesn't it?" You could see guys getting more and more nervous as cards were drawn and theirs still hadn't been. We had some serious appetites then, and if you tossed in some high-end wine, the bill could get pretty steep, so some guys took this game pretty seriously. Some of us could laugh it off, but I saw more than one guy get really upset when he was on the hook for a meal.

Fans may not realize this, but there are a lot of cheap guys in the NHL. You'd see flashes of it as guys got nervous playing credit card roulette, but it was even clearer when it came to tipping the trainers. The trainers are the unsung heroes on every sports team. They take care of you every day of the season. They fix your skates, transport your equipment, and wash your dirty laundry for eighty-two games. They keep you healthy and fit, and they look after your smallest needs. A thankless job. A real pro recognizes that and takes care of the trainers at the end of the season. Unfortunately, some guys were just clueless and didn't show that kind of consideration. Nothing pissed me off more.

While being part of a team is a ton of fun most times, there is a serious side to it as well. In the NHL, there's an unspoken code—certain things that are just understood to be off-limits when you're part of a team. As a young player, you need to learn the ropes, but you get a feel for them pretty quickly.

Over the years, a lot of pro athletes, myself included, can find themselves in delicate situations or with the opportunity to make a decision that could hurt other people. I lost my virginity when I was fourteen, while I was playing Junior C with a bunch of twenty-year-olds. It was so crazy back then that, at only fourteen or fifteen years old, I was going into bars with the older guys on the team without ever having to show any ID. Being a young guy, that was a lot of fun, but it made it hard sometimes to keep my head on straight and remember where I'd come from. As I got older, I smartened up, and throughout my NHL career, I never had a thought of betraying a teammate's trust. I always remembered the code. And I can go to my grave with that.

Despite the problems some guys might cause, for the most part being part of a team in the NHL was amazing. There are so many different characters from different backgrounds in the same dressing room day after day. When you spend that much time with the same bunch of guys, you really get to know what they are all about. One of my favourite teammates during my NHL career was Glenn Healy. Heals was always quick with the one-liners. Most guys couldn't keep up with him when it came to the jokes, but I buried him when I wanted to. We'd trade zingers back and forth, and I'd keep it going as long as I could because I used to love to hear his comebacks.

Later in my career, I was the one who brought up Glenn Healy's name when the Leafs were searching for a general manager. He was my choice ahead of John Ferguson Jr. or any of the other guys on the team's short list. The media's response was insulting—they laughed at the idea. They didn't take him seriously. Now he's a colour commentator, the most articulate guy on television, and picks up things during a game that nobody else sees. The best in the business. Heals just says it the way it is, and he's found great success.

When we were teammates in Toronto, Heals admitted to me that he didn't like me at all when we were opponents. But once I started playing in Toronto, that changed. We became fiercely loyal to one another. The turning point came during the 1997–98 season. We were playing in New Jersey, and there was a faceoff outside of the dot in the neutral zone in front of our bench. Healy wasn't playing that game, so he was sitting on the far end of our bench when I noticed Krzysztof Oliwa from the Devils saying something to him. My immediate reaction was to get upset because I thought Oliwa was chirping our bench. As far as I was concerned, you never did that. So right after that, I switched wings, the puck was dropped, and I fought Oliwa. After the game, we were on the bus when Healy came up to me and said, "Tie, we were just wishing each other a Merry Christmas." I looked at Heals and said, "He still shouldn't be talking to our bench."

* * *

One of the special things about playing in the NHL is that you get the chance to meet athletes from other sports. Back in the Chicago Bulls' heyday, when they were on top of the sports world, they were in Toronto to play the Raptors. At the time, Michael Jordan was the absolute king. By chance, my then wife, Leanne, and I were out with a few other friends at the same place that the Bulls were after their game. I was playing pool at the back of the place when, all of a sudden, MJ walked up and asked to play a game against me. I had met Michael once or twice before, but we didn't know each other very well. But I said yes, of course, and joked that we should wager something to make the game more interesting.

This was back when you could still smoke in bars, so we both had big cigars in our mouths, and a crowd formed around us as we set up the balls. As we started playing, I got lucky early on with some easy shots. But before long, Jordan had only six balls left, and as the crowd around us quieted, he said to me, "If I sink all these, then you have to bring your son to the game tomorrow."

MJ proceeded to clean the table, took a big puff on his cigar, and then threw his pool cue on the table. He looked at me and just said, "See you and your son tomorrow; tickets will be at Will Call."

When my son, Max, and I got to the stadium the next day, we discovered that Jordan had left us courtside seats! Max was young at the time, and he was in awe of everything. Well, doesn't MJ hit a three-pointer right in front of us and give us a wink and six-shooter with a smile. Max couldn't take his eyes off Jordan, not knowing he was watching the best basketball player on the planet. Afterwards, Jordan told me to come to the locker room with Max. MJ came and met us with a towel on, and he grabbed Max and walked around with him on his arm. Max ended up getting his picture taken with all of the Bulls players. The funniest moment was when Dennis Rodman held Max for a picture and Max just bawled his eyes out! Years later, at Chris Chelios's Hall of Fame party, I saw Michael again, and I thanked him for what he did for Max. Being a class act, MJ remembered meeting Max, and of course, he remembered the pool game, too.

I put Michael Jordan in the same category as all my sports idols. My sports heroes all had one thing in common: they were all winners. I was a fan of Jordan, Magic Johnson, and Larry Bird in basketball. In hockey, right from a young age, I loved the Montreal Canadiens, especially Guy Lafleur and Larry Robinson. Later it was the Islanders, with Bryan Trottier and Denis Potvin. And after that, it was the Oilers dynasty of Wayne Gretzky, Mark Messier, and Paul Coffey. Even as a young kid, I was a Yankees fan. I loved Reggie Jackson and Don Mattingly. Later on, it was Kirk Gibson, Lou Whitaker, Alan Trammell, and the Detroit Tigers. When I watched football, I wanted to see Walter Payton and Tony Dorsett, and when it came to soccer, I was all about Pelé and Diego Maradona. And my favourite tennis players were John McEnroe and Björn Borg.

I am a sports fanatic at heart, so these were the guys that I wanted to be like. All of them were winners who competed every time they touched the ice, field, or court. They inspired me as a kid, and they continued to inspire me even when I was a pro myself. They were all great athletes by themselves, but they were also respected, team-first guys, and I learned from them just by watching.

* * *

The key to surviving in the show was being mentally tough. The NHL is all about the survival of the fittest, and part of my system was to intimidate the other team's players during the warm-up.

My routine started before I even stepped on the ice. As I got ready in the dressing room, the Leafs trainers would hand me half a cup of Coke, and they'd unwrap and leave out three pieces of gum for me. The trainers were amazing. They showed us such care and paid attention to every detail—for example, the wrappers on the gum were always peeled back so that I could just grab the gum as I walked past and toss it into my mouth before I hit the ice. I figured that if I was chewing gum as I warmed up, it would make me look cockier, which would help to rattle the players on the other team.

Once I was on the rink, I would stretch at centre ice and stare down the other team, especially their tough guy, to get them thinking about what I might do to them that night. The stare down had a purpose: I wanted everyone on the other team to know I was watching. I thrived on those mind games. And the best part of all is that I was calm and controlled the whole time, even as my opponents became rattled. I made sure that the other players all knew where I was and that they were all wondering what I was thinking. I would also make sure that I was the last guy on the ice for the warm-up. Sometimes I delayed going out a little bit so I could really mess with them. That way, when I finally did get on the ice, I could see and feel all of the players on the other team turn to look at me. That's when I knew I was inside their heads. That was true for the first half of my career, at least. Later, when I started to become a better-conditioned and more mature player, warm-ups were shorter and we didn't have as much time on the ice, so I would do more active warm-ups. Of course, at that point, I didn't feel the need to prove myself to others the same way that I did early in my career.

That routine ended up being the reason I met Mario Lemieux. It was during a warm-up at Madison Square Garden in the 1991–92 season. I was stretching at centre ice, staring down the Penguins' tough guys, and Mario was skating around. I looked over at him at one point, for no other reason than because he's Mario Lemieux and he was already a legend. As he skated by me, Mario saw me looking and said something to me that I couldn't quite make out. I kept stretching, thinking that he was trying to chirp me. He kept skating around, and I could see he was laughing the whole way around, and then he finally stopped, leaned against the boards, and said, "No, seriously, Tie: can you get me and ten of my teammates into the China Club?"

It wasn't what I was expecting to hear, so all I could say was, "Yeah."

In the early 1990s, the China Club was the hottest nightclub in Manhattan. It was almost impossible to get in on a normal night, no matter who you were. I had been there a few times, and I'd become friends with one of the bouncers there, Johnny B. I treated him like a normal guy, and we got to know each other well. So whenever I showed up, I would walk past all the celebrities lined up outside, hug Johnny and the other bouncers in their black leather coats, and head right in. This was in the day when Mike Tyson was the boxer to beat and Mark Wahlberg was Marky Mark. Those were the sorts of guys you'd meet at the China Club.

I really liked watching Mike Tyson fight. He wasn't a tall guy—roughly the same height as me—but he was fearless. I was heavily influenced by him and other greats like Sugar Ray Leonard, Marvin Hagler, Thomas "the Hitman" Hearns, and Roberto Duran. They were all smart fighters and warriors, and I got my fighting edge by watching those five in action during their heyday. At the club, though, Tyson was very generous. He would buy champagne—Cristal and Rosé—for everyone in the VIP section. We're talking thirty to forty bottles, and Tyson would cover all of it. He wasn't a sociable guy, but still, he'd be surrounded by people and he'd pay for drinks for all of them.

Mark Wahlberg was a little different. I met Mark for the first time at the China Club. This was back before he was a movie star. I don't think Mark was much of a hockey fan or that he knew who I was at the time—to this day, if a Boston team is winning, Mark suddenly becomes an expert in the sport. But someone must have told Mark I was a tough guy with the Rangers, because he approached me at the club so respectfully. As I shook his hand for the first time, I could tell he was going to be something special.

The Penguins smoked us 5–2 in the game, including two goals and an assist by Mario, so we had a closed-door team meeting. I was still in my hockey pants and skates when we finished. All of a sudden, the dressing room door opened and the media and everyone else came flooding in. In the commotion, a security guard came up to me and said, "Hey, Tie, Mario Lemieux is at the door." I had no idea Mario would be ready that quickly, but there he was, already showered, with his hair gelled and everything.

"So, we all set?" he asked. "You're going to come for a drink, right?"

I wasn't sure I wanted to go out that night, but I ended up going with Brian Leetch because he was friends with Kevin Stevens, who was with the Penguins at the time. We got to the China Club, and the Penguins players went off and did their own thing. I talked to Mario a little bit that night, but that was about it. Nothing special really seemed to come of it, and we all went our separate ways at the end of the night.

I would often run into guys from other teams at the China Club. One night in my first season with New York, I was at the club with a bunch of my Rangers teammates when we ran into a group of players from the New Jersey Devils. One of the Devils' defencemen, Ken Daneyko, knew Mark Messier from when they were growing up in Alberta. The two of them were chirping each other back and forth. Suddenly Messier yelled out to Ken, "Hey, this kid can beat you in an arm wrestle!" and he pointed to me.

Ken was a big, strong guy, and as we got set up at the table, his teammates were talking to each other about how quickly he'd beat me. Ken insisted on betting on it, so there was a hundred dollars on the table. Well, I won the first round. And then the second. Then we switched hands and I beat Ken with my left hand, too. I would let him get three-quarters of the way to winning, and then, just when he thought he had me, I'd crank his arm back and slam his hand down to win the round.

Ken got more and more frustrated as we went, and he was doing shots of Jägermeister and tequila the whole time. When he'd finally tired of losing arm-wrestling matches, Ken shouted, "Let's head-butt!" I really didn't want to head-butt Ken, but he wouldn't take no for an answer. Things didn't go the way that Ken planned, though, and the next thing you know, he had a massive goose egg on his forehead and I was still standing. The next time we played New Jersey, I was in the dressing room when Messier approached me with an envelope with my name on it. Inside was a hundred-dollar bill that Ken had sent over. We were all a little nuts back then, but in a good way.

After my fight with Bob Probert, I took my time in New York more seriously, and I started travelling to Los Angeles to get away to somewhere nobody knew me. It turned out that Mario did the same thing, and as we spent years travelling and training together, we just kind of hit it off. We had a lot of laughs. It's amazing that that happened, really, because he was the best player in the world and then there was me. We were polar opposites and we never played together, but we bonded right away.

It still amazes me when I think of what Mario had to put up with during his playing career and afterwards. The adversity that he has faced in his life—his bad back, battling cancer, his hip—

makes you imagine what he could have done if he'd been healthy his whole career. But through it all, he never changed who he was; he never stopped being the same humble guy he had always been. Once, we travelled to meet some old friends in Phoenix. When we got to our rental vehicle at the airport, there were three rows of seats in the car, and Mario climbed into the back with me. Mario is a tall guy, so you can imagine how long his legs are. The other guys tried to get Mario to change places, but Mario insisted on staying in the back. He felt that they had seniority on him, and that meant he would put them before himself to show courtesy. Mario's constant selflessness shows just how humble he is, and it's why I respect him so much.

Every time I was a free agent in my career, the Penguins' general manager, Craig Patrick, would try to sign me to his team. When I retired from the Leafs, he even offered me a three-year contract. But I wanted to retire as a Leaf. Mario, being one of my best friends, understood my decision and respected it. There's no BS in my friendships with Mats and Mario. I don't kiss their butts, and I don't want anything from either one of them. They know what I'm all about.

Even though I have been good friends with both Mats and Mario, the two never really spent any time with each other until the summer of 2014, when the three of us travelled together. Mario is one of Mats's idols, and he had no idea that Mario was going to be on the trip, so for the first day, Mats was completely starstruck. Mats still looked up to Mario, after all those years. To get Mats over his first-day shyness, I introduced him to the "Joker." Mario calls me the "Joke" and I call him the "Joker." I warned Mats that, just when you think Mario's not paying attention, he'll hit you with a joke or tease you. Sure enough, by about the second day, Mario started giving Mats the business, and that relaxed Mats. By the third day, Mats was starting to get so comfortable, you couldn't shut him up!

When I think of guys like Mats and Mario and their place in hockey's history, and I think about my connection to them, I think about accountability. Since I was the toughest guy on whatever team I played on, I made people accountable every night. I told that to Mario once, and he said, "Yeah, but we were accountable to eighteen thousand fans every night." And in a lot of ways, Mario was right, because guys like him were the entertainment. They won games, and they were the players fans paid to see. But at the same time, they were the best players, so they didn't have to deal with every single little thing on the ice or in the dressing room. That was a job for someone like me.

Mats and Mario are both Hall of Famers, two of the NHL's all-time greats. Other than my fighting record, the closest I'll get to the Hall of Fame is my flip pass to Selänne on his rookie record-breaking goal. Those two guys took care of me, and they were — and still are — always there for me. There is a huge comfort factor with both of them. Even though Mats and Mario come from different countries and different backgrounds, they both have similar traits that I have always admired: they are respectful, loyal, and humble. Everything they do in life, they do with a sense of humility. Mats and Mario are still two of my closest hockey friends, and they always will be. And at the end of the day, that is what it's all about, because my friends and my family are everything to me.

* * *

Whenever I get a chance to meet NHL alumni, I see it as an opportunity to show my appreciation and respect. I think that sort of attitude should be automatic when you meet guys like the Hull brothers, Ron Ellis, and Red Kelly. They are always so kind and so positive when you meet them. I have enormous respect and admiration for the legends of the NHL. It is always humbling to meet them, and even more so if they tell me they were a fan of the way I played the game.

Montreal Canadiens defenceman Guy Lapointe had his number retired by the team in 2014. It was a great evening worthy of a great player. I watched the ceremony, and I cried because I was so happy to see a man that I'd met honoured the right way. One night, in Max's first year with the London Knights, I was in town watching him play, and afterwards I went to Joe Kool's, a popular hangout that's usually packed on game nights. This particular night, as I walked in, the bouncer told me, "Guy Lapointe's here."

"Where?" I asked. "Bring me to him."

I always feel it's my responsibility to go to these sorts of legends, rather than assume they'll recognize or come to me. So I went over to Lapointe and introduced myself. He said, "I know exactly who you are. I followed your career and I am a fan." Later in our conversation, Lapointe also said, "I respect what you did." Here I was, trying to meet Lapointe and tell him that I was a huge fan of *his* while I was growing up, and he turned it around and said he was a fan of mine. That is what I call being humble.

My original blueprint on how to be a winner in hockey goes back to the Montreal Canadiens of the 1970s. They were what everyone in hockey always wanted to be because they knew how to win. As time passed, that blueprint was adopted by the Islanders, and then the Oilers, Penguins, and Red Wings, all of whom inherited and built on the Canadiens' legacy.

More than just winning, the Montreal Canadiens always seemed to carry themselves with such class. Jean Béliveau was the classiest of them all, and he set the tone for generations of Canadiens players. Béliveau taught me that, no matter what, it is always the right choice to acknowledge the people around you and show respect.

One of the highlights from my time in Winnipeg was when I was fortunate enough to meet Béliveau. He had come to Winnipeg for a book signing, and I waited in line with Leanne, then my wife, to get my copy of his book autographed. I was only twenty-three years old, and I can still remember my excitement. When I finally reached Béliveau at the table, I couldn't believe how big he was. He had such presence—the definition of larger than life. I was surprised to find that he recognized me right away. We had a very friendly chat, and from that point on, for the rest of my career, anytime I played in Montreal and Béliveau was in the building, he would make a point of coming to our dressing room before the game to say hello. I don't think there's anyone in professional sports like Béliveau; he was in a league of his own. His death in December 2014 was a great loss for the sports world. The Montreal Canadiens are all class, and so many classy guys have worn that uniform. A lot of teams and players across the NHL could learn from the way they did things.

I always felt there were two types of players in an NHL dressing room: the phonies and the warriors. The phonies were anybody in the dressing room who talked behind guys' backs or who only cared about themselves. The warriors were the complete opposite: they were the kind of guys who would do anything to win. They would do anything to support you and they would never stab you in the back. Luckily, the majority of guys were in the second category. Hockey is like everything else: the majority of people are good, but the ones that are clueless, you can't change them.

I could instantly tell the phonies and the warriors apart in a dressing room. I had a feel for them all. Still, it didn't change my job or what I had to do. I had to protect every guy on the team, no matter who they were or what they were like. When I was first entering the NHL, the older players always taught the younger ones. The guys who had common sense and a positive attitude were the guys who passed the torch. When I was a veteran, I did the same thing with my younger teammates.

As far as modern players are concerned, I am a big fan of Montreal's P. K. Subban. He's a modern warrior. Subban has been a family friend for a long time, and he grew up in a tough part of Toronto. Now he has a $72 million contract. Early in his career, Subban asked for my advice about how to be a good teammate and how to best show leadership in the dressing room. I was impressed by Subban's maturity. He's a young, talented athlete, but he was humble and respectful enough to ask for advice. After Subban signed his big contract, I told him that he was the new face of the Montreal Canadiens. I told him, "Now you *are* Jean Béliveau. You *are* Rocket Richard. That is you now for the next eight years."

The people you meet in the game are incredible. I am humbled when I think about the lifelong friendships I made that all circle back to hockey. I have a special bond with the guys I played with that is different from the connection I have with a lot of my other friends. We had good times, and we also had bad times, but we were able to survive all those ups and downs because, no matter where we were, we stuck together as a team. And that's why hockey is so special. When you're playing the game, it's your livelihood, not your life. It's an even bigger business now than when I was in the game. A career goes by quickly, so you have to enjoy every day that you have with your teammates. Because when it stops, it stops.

10

Last Days in the NHL

JOHN FERGUSON JR. took over as the general manager of the Leafs in August 2003, the year before the lockout. He was thirty-six years old and had never been a general manager before that. I didn't talk to him a lot at first, and I didn't have much of a problem with him in the beginning, either. The real problems started after the lockout ended, just before the 2005–2006 season. Larry Tanenbaum, a part owner of the Leafs and a close family friend, told Mats and me that he wanted us to meet Ferguson before the season to get our opinion about free agents. So we met at my new house.

Stupid me. I had just built my dream home. Glenn Healy called it the "Taj Mah-Domi." I planned on living in it the rest of my life. Mats and I were there when Ferguson arrived. I opened the door, and as he walked into the house, he was stone cold. He looked around, scoping out the place—not in a friendly way—and asked, "Is this all from hockey money?" The way he said that, it sounded to me as though he didn't think I'd be making money from hockey much longer. Or at least, not as a Leaf. I knew right away that we weren't going to have a good ending. He just wasn't my type of guy.

Ferguson gave Mats and me a list of free agents divided into grades A, B, and C. Mats and I looked over the names, trying to figure out who would fit best on the team and who would bring the skills we needed. We highlighted the names that we thought would be the best ones to sign for the team, and he left with that. Over the next few weeks, Ferguson started the free-agent signing process, and every acquisition he made surprised us. He didn't sign a single player that Mats and I had recommended, and everyone that we told him not to go after, he ended up signing. I don't know whether he tried to get any of the names on our list, but as the pieces fell into place, I knew that my career in Toronto was coming to an end. I just knew. For the past decade, Mats and I had led the team. And now it was all coming apart.

Ferguson didn't seem to like how popular I was with everyone—not just with teammates, but also with coaches, trainers, and all of the arena staff at the ACC. Because of the lessons I had learned from my dad when I was young, I have always been the kind of guy who enjoys taking the time to talk to everyone—the parking lot attendants, the security guards, the ice crew, you name it. I talked to anyone and everyone, and over the years, I treated everyone like family. But I started to get the sense that Ferguson didn't like my reputation around the arena. I think he was insecure with me around; maybe he felt I was a threat. My street smarts were at work, and those instincts had never let me down.

Usually, if I had a problem with someone, I was vocal about it. Guys always knew where they stood with me because, if I was ever pissed off at someone, I made sure they knew about it. But my father had always said, "Never show your cards—to anybody," and he lived what he preached.

Before he died, Dad had regularly been going to doctor appointments by himself. He told us it was to manage his high blood sugar; it turned out he'd been going to see a cardiologist the whole time. The doctor had diagnosed him with a serious heart condition and informed him that the only thing that would save him would be a heart transplant. Most people would bring that sort of news back to their family right away. But my dad was the opposite. He decided not to have the surgery, and he didn't tell any of us about his condition. He kept going on with his day-to-day routines, smiling and making us all laugh right to the very end.

I sometimes found it hard to live up to the example my dad had set. Some guys didn't like how direct I could be, but I've never pulled any punches. Still, the problems I sensed that Ferguson had with me were different from the usual challenges I faced. So I kept my dad's words in my mind and tried to fly under the radar.

But the problems only got worse in the 2005–2006 season. The summer before, a player from another team had contacted me. He had once begged to come over to my house to talk about getting signed by the Leafs. He knew all about my relationship with Larry Tanenbaum, and he wanted me to use that connection to help him get signed in Toronto. I heard the guy out, and then I went to bat for him. Eventually, Ferguson signed the guy.

Later that season, Mats was taken out of the lineup with an injury, and in some games after that, I found myself playing on a line with this other player. We were winning games, and I knew I had to keep playing hard and being successful if I was going to be able to make it through the situation I was in. I wasn't going to let jealousies or fears affect me—I would continue to be a good team-mate and keep helping the Leafs win games. But then, after a brief bit of success, suddenly and for no apparent reason I was demoted to the fourth line. I have always prided myself on being mentally tough and being a good teammate, but I found myself being tested in unprecedented ways during that time. All of the strategies and tools I'd used to endure hundreds of challenges and fights in the past weren't much help in dealing with a guy who had so much control over my career. We were playing on an uneven field.

I was struggling, and I looked for guidance from the people around me who I trusted. It was times like that when I missed my dad most. With my dad gone, Don Cherry became like a second father figure to me. Anytime I had a problem, I knew I could pick up the phone to call Don and that he would be there to listen and give me his advice. I relied on him and a few others for support as I tried to make sense of what I was going through.

But despite the help that I had, things went from bad to worse. Pretty soon, the player I had helped bring to Toronto started acting out. It was like he couldn't take the pressure. Then he went down with an injury. He was sitting some games, and the team was strug-gling, and eventually things came to a head at a team meeting. This guy stood up in front of the team and started criticizing the guys around him. He talked as though he knew all the answers, and he acted as though everyone else was the problem. We were stunned, and he just kept going on and on. A lot of my teammates were staring at me in shock. Mats looked at me as if to say, "Do something. Now."

"Hey!" I yelled. "Why don't you shut the hell up? If you don't have anything good to say, don't say it. We don't need any negative

BS right now. I don't know what kind of leadership you learned on other teams, because you don't have any."

At this time, I was one of the Leafs' most experienced players. I was one of the core guys, and I'd tried to teach everyone the same values that Mark Messier had taught me when I was young. Some guys had caught on, while some guys hadn't or only cared about themselves. The guys who understood me knew that we had to be a tight team if we wanted to win. Mats and I had been the leaders on the Leafs team for ten years. Over that period, a lot of great guys had come and gone, but we kept the team on the right track. We were fortunate enough to play with some really great players — like Gary Roberts, Joe Nieuwendyk, and Alex Mogilny — towards the ends of their careers. We created a special atmosphere where everyone was welcome and where the focus was on winning as a team. We couldn't let any negativity enter the room. But after that incident, the dressing room started to break up. Guys started drifting apart, and the chemistry just wasn't there. And at the higher levels, I felt like there was no effort to build the team in the right way. That 2005–2006 season wore me down mentally. Everything we'd been working so hard to build seemed to be going south fast, and I was in a position where, no matter what I did, I wasn't going to get an opportunity to help.

One game in late October of that season stands out. We played the Senators, and we lost badly that night. By the second period, the Sens were already up 4–0, and they went on to win 8–0. I was playing on the fourth line that night, and I wasn't happy about it. Brian McGrattan on the Sens kept asking me for a fight. Wade Belak and Nathan Perrott — two other tough guys on the Leafs at that time — were also dressed that night, but they didn't want to fight him. Finally my frustration got the better of me and I said, "Let's go."

It was a mistake. I wasn't mentally sharp and I wasn't into the game that night. Already, I could feel that I was being pushed out of the Leafs organization, and it got in my head. I wasn't ready to fight that night—I wasn't calm and my head wasn't in it, so my guard was down. As McGrattan and I fought, I realized he had worked a hand free when I was holding a jersey with no arm in it. I could see his fist coming. It wasn't a very hard punch, and it didn't hurt me, but he cut me. And with the amount of blood that he drew, everyone thought he really nailed me. As I skated to the penalty box, I wondered if things could get any worse.

But the problems kept coming. I was one of the most loyal guys there was to Pat Quinn, so I never blamed him for what happened to me that year. I knew that whatever was going on with me in the lineup had nothing to do with him. The low point of that year came on March 23, 2006, when we were in Montreal to play the Canadiens, our biggest rivals. Before the game, Pat called me into his office, sat me down, and told me I would be a healthy scratch that night. I could tell he felt bad about doing it, but he was going to dress a Russian kid, Alexander Suglobov, instead of me. I was stunned for a number of reasons, but I was most shocked that Pat was going to do this in Montreal, of all places. He knew I played my best games as a Maple Leaf against the Canadiens. The excitement around those games and the atmosphere in Montreal is beyond anything you could imagine, and it always brought out the best in me.

I told Pat, "I know this isn't you making this decision, but if we don't make the playoffs, you and I will both be out of here. I can help. I know the history and tradition. This kid you're putting in for me can't be expected to have a clue."

Our season was on the line. When we were in Montreal, we only needed to win a few more games to secure a spot in the playoffs. Pat Quinn knew that, but the decision was out of his hands. So Suglobov started the game on the top line with Mats Sundin. When Mats found out I wasn't playing, he was pissed. He knew I could have made a difference that night; just my presence in the dressing room might have helped.

Well, we lost 5–1 that night. That was the beginning of the end. A few weeks later, the regular season came to a close, and sure enough, we missed the playoffs by two points. And not long after that, despite guys on the team coming out and publicly supporting him, Pat was fired.

Years later, well after my career was over, Pat and I ran into each other at the funeral of a mutual friend. After we'd caught up a bit, we got to talking about the end of that season. Pat got very emotional, and he said, "Son, I owe you an apology. And I don't do this for everyone. You were right, and I'm sorry."

I told him, "Hey, I appreciate that you apologized, and I love you." I knew it wasn't his fault. Pat Quinn always used his good judgment, but this was a case where he had to go against his own rules, and I knew that it bothered him. For Pat, a stubborn Irish guy, to admit to an error like that was big, and I respected his heart and his honesty.

After that season, I could tell my days with the Leafs were coming to an end. I don't believe in holding grudges, but I have no time for guys who think they are the company or they are the brand. One thing you learn as an athlete is that the name on the front of the jersey is all that matters. And that name on the front of the jersey will be there a lot longer than any name on the back. Some guys don't realize that, or when they do, it's usually too late. It's about being a real person and a team player, no matter what your title or your role. That, and what you do for your teammates and fans on and off the ice, is what you're remembered for.

But sometimes, a new person will arrive and try to make their own footprint. That's exactly what I saw happening with Ferguson. When he took over as general manager, everyone was excited about how smart and educated he was—they thought he was just what the Leafs needed. But, as it turned out, he made so many mistakes that the Leafs are still paying for them. He might have been book smart, but that didn't mean he showed common sense.

At the same time that Pat Quinn was fired, Ferguson bought out my contract. Mats tried to intervene; he told Ferguson that he needed me there to help preserve the chemistry that had worked so well for us for so many years up to that point. But Ferguson didn't buy it; he didn't seem to see what the team was or how Mats and I worked together. Maybe, to him, it was a hockey decision. To me, it was a personal issue. Either way, I had no control over it.

When I was bought out, I didn't ever ask Larry Tanenbaum to step in and intervene. Everyone's career comes to an end at some point, and some guys are unwilling—or unable—to accept that. But that wasn't me. I didn't take it out on the rest of the team. I carried on quietly and confidently with my head held high, just like my dad taught me. After I retired, the Penguins offered me a three-year contract. But my mind was made up—I wanted to retire as a Leaf. I had seen what happened with Dougie Gilmour, Wendel Clark, and CuJo. I had watched these guys, who deserved every success and had worked hard for years, sign new deals or get traded late in their careers to try to win a Cup with another team, only to fall short, find themselves with reduced roles, or get injured. I didn't want that to happen to me. I wanted to go with as much dignity as I could, and I wanted to retire as a Maple Leaf—I couldn't see myself wearing any other jersey after that. After sixteen years and 1,020 games in the NHL, it was time. I'd had my moment in the spotlight and enjoyed my life in the NHL. But everything eventually has to end and it was time to move on with the next chapter in my life.

11

Keeping It Real

M Y OFFICIAL height in NHL media and information guides was listed as five feet, ten inches, well south of the league average. Maybe it's because I was always smaller than the people I competed against, or maybe it's because of the way I was raised, but I've always believed that you need to stand up for the little guy in all walks of life.

I can't stand rude people. I can't stand people who keep talking on their phones while they're placing an order at the coffee shop or who don't even acknowledge the men and women at airport security. I can't stand people who refuse to tip doormen, servers, and porters. Basically, I hate it when people lack common courtesy. What I'm talking about goes beyond what it takes to be a good pro in the NHL. This is all about what it takes to be a good person in everyday life and how to connect to people in the right way.

I am a firm believer in treating all people from all walks of life the same way, respecting and acknowledging whatever they do, and sometimes even getting to know them personally when I have the opportunity. To me, it doesn't matter if you're the shoeshine guy or the car wash attendant or the coffee shop employee; everybody is important in life. Every job is a good job and when you do it to the best of your ability, that deserves respect. I once stopped and talked for twenty minutes to a guy whose job was to hand out towels in the bathroom. You'd be amazed what he sees and hears. I'd rather talk to the men and women on the factory floor than their management any day. I always learn something new when I stop to talk or have coffee with construction workers I meet on their breaks. These are the people who know the true meaning of working for a living.

I have the utmost respect for my buddy Milton, who works as a waiter at the Four Seasons hotel in New York. He's been there for over twenty years, and every time I see Milton, he is smiling and happy. "I'm in the service business, Mr. Domi. I have to perform if I want to be the best." Milton always tells me that it is his job to treat everybody equally, no matter who they are. And he sees all types. I admire people like Milton who spend all day serving others and who can stay so positive throughout it. The lessons he lives by are the same ones I learned growing up through the NHL. We think the same way.

Milton told me that when we first met, he had no idea who I was and didn't know anything about hockey, let alone my NHL career. After I left, some of his coworkers pulled him aside and asked, "Do you know who you were talking to?" Milton didn't, but he also didn't care—to him, I was just Mr. Domi, another person to be treated with respect like any other.

I once asked Milton what his formula was for being so happy every day. He said to me, "In the service business, my first impression and my last impression are what's most important. You know when you put on your uniform?"

"Yeah," I replied.

He proudly grabbed the Four Seasons name tag on his vest and said, "When I put on *my* uniform, I have to treat everyone like they are special, because they are."

Another guy at the Four Seasons whom I admire is Joe, the bellman. I admire all the bellmen there, but I've known Joe for years. I once watched Joe—in the freezing New York cold—load ten bags onto a cart with no gloves or coat. As the guests got out of the truck he was unloading, not one of them looked at Joe, let alone thanked or tipped him, as they ran into the hotel to warm up. But it didn't get to Joe. He stayed upbeat and positive, with a smile on his face as he did his job. When he came in, I said, "Joe, nobody even acknowledged you there. Are you okay?"

"Tie," he responded, "I love my job. I've been doing this for twenty-five years. I don't expect anything from anybody. As a matter of fact, I don't even expect anything from my parents. They have to insist on taking me to dinner on my birthday, and we still fight over the cheque."

I know what all of these people are going through every day as they work hard to make a living and feed their families. My dad owned and ran a coin-operated laundry, a variety store, and a number of restaurants. He had to deal with people every day to make a living, and no matter how tired he was or what struggles he was going through, he was always smiling and always happy. I see my dad in all of these people.

I was once in a coffee shop—one of those really cool new shops in the SoHo neighbourhood of Manhattan that's always busy—and I noticed that there was a big jar on the counter full of tips. I told the people working there, "Wow, you guys must be great!" The guy and the girl behind the counter were both so accommodating and happy. So I tipped them well. They thanked me, but I stopped them and replied, "No, thank *you* so much. Your positive energy and the way you work it are very impressive. That's why your jar is so full."

Then the guy after me ordered, and he was an obnoxious jerk. He was on his phone the whole time. The employee at the counter was trying to get the order right while this jerk just put his finger up, gesturing for the kid to hold on a minute, even though the line was building up behind him. He snapped his order at the employee and then went back to his phone call. While this was happening, I was standing a few feet away, adding some cream to my coffee. I watched the kid at the counter stay patient, and the whole time, he went out of his way to be nice. But when the guy on the phone finally got his coffee, he walked off without even saying thank you—forget about tipping them. I went back to the counter and apologized for the guy's behaviour.

The kid behind the counter looked at me and asked, "Who are you?"

I told him, "I'm just an ex-hockey player, an old ex-hockey player."

I kept going back to that coffee shop, and over time I got to know the people who worked there. Tony is one of the guys who runs the place, and I always take time to talk to him whenever I'm there. He has three huge Gothic letters tattooed on his right forearm: *P*, *M*, and *A*. They stand for "positive mental attitude." Tony appreciates talking about life and everyday things, as opposed to most of his conversations at work, which tend to be about coffee and milk and not much else.

I can't believe how rude some people are to him. He tells me, "You have no idea. That happens every day. We are the busiest

coffee shop in SoHo and probably every tenth person is like that."
Think about that—one out of every ten people is rude! Tony is
used to seeing people refuse to stop talking on their phone or even
look at him while they place their order. He tried to explain it away
to me, telling me that this is Manhattan and everybody is hustling
and busy and nobody has time for anything, least of all looking at
you and being polite. Tony is a better person than I am to excuse
that kind of behaviour, because I sure don't. If a person can't be
bothered to treat others like they're individuals and important in
their own right, I don't want them around me.

What drives me nuts is that I went through some tough times
and didn't ever want to be negative or show my stress. Especially
the guys I got to know over the years who worked in my apartment
building. I know that the people who work there have families at
home to feed and are doing what they can because it's tough out
there to make a living. And whatever it is they do, they do it with
the right attitude every day. Nigel, the concierge in my building,
is a perfect example of that. I've gotten to know Nigel, as well as
each and every person who works there, over the years. They're all
special and have always had my back, so I treat them all like family, making sure to say hello and to acknowledge them when I walk
out and walk in. It's literally the least I can do.

Every year, I rent a private box at a Raptors game for everyone
who works in my building—it's my way of thanking them for their
hard work. These people valet cars, help with groceries, you name
it. But the residents don't recognize the work these people do; they
don't tip them or even greet them as they go past. I'm shocked
at the way I see some residents in my building act—how cheap,
entitled, and rude they can be. I see them order these employees
around like they're their butlers. What's worse is that they're not

polite and don't display any decent manners towards these hard-working people. That upsets me, and I admire how they handle it—they get treated like shit, but they don't complain and they do their jobs better than anyone.

The same goes for the parking lot attendants and security guards in London, Ontario. For four years, every time I went to watch Max play for the Knights, I would bring coffee for these people before the game. They took care of my son and saw him every day, and they always had the nicest things to say about him—hearing those kind words made me prouder than winning any championship ever could.

I'm constantly impressed by how hard some people will work for a living, and how much they'll sacrifice. The winter in 2014 was awful in Toronto, and nowhere was that clearer than at the car wash I go to. Every day was colder than the last, and these poor guys would be out there, cleaning their clients' cars. I showed up there on one of the most brutal days that winter; it was cold and windy, just nasty. I saw all of the car owners sitting under the heaters, warm and cozy, while these poor employees were trying to keep their hands and feet from freezing while they dried down cars. I spent some time with the cleaners, trying to take their mind off the cold, before I went over to warm up. Outside the office was a wooden, yellow toolbox that they'd turned into a tip jar, and I noticed nobody was putting anything in it. So, loud enough for everyone to hear, I yelled out, "Hey, guys! Where's the tip jar?" I made sure all of the people under the heaters heard me, and then I made a show of walking over to the toolbox and putting a bill in. The people around me caught on and some reluctantly started to dig into their wallets and purses to put a little something in the tip jar. The sad thing is that if I hadn't said anything, most of the people there wouldn't have even bothered giving these poor, frozen guys at the car wash a proper "thank you" or a decent tip.

I just don't understand why other people don't think of others the same way they think of themselves. Why can't everyone treat people equally and with respect? Sometimes a simple "please" and "thank you" is all you need to make someone's day. That's how I was brought up. Small gestures—like shaking someone's hand or looking them in the eye when you greet them—are important. If we can't make the effort to do even those smallest of things for each other, how can we really show each other the respect we all deserve?

* * *

I have a buddy whom I have gotten to know over my years of travelling in New York City. His name is Rod, and he works every day from 7 a.m. to 7 p.m. at the Waldorf Astoria, in a room that is no more than three metres by two metres in size. He gets up before dawn every day to take the train into work, and then he gets home late after shining shoes all day. Rod is in that little room, shining shoes, six days a week. Rod is also the best at what he does.

I know for a fact that the first time I went to see Rod to get my shoes shined, he had no clue who I was. We were talking when an older lady came in to get her shoes shined as well. I was so impressed with Rod and how polite and positive he was—he could talk as easily with the other woman as he could with me. I had been to see Rod at least four more times after that day before someone at the Waldorf Astoria told him who I was. I liked the fact that he didn't know I was a former hockey player. I was just "Tie," another anonymous guy who came in to get his shoes shined. I was always entertained by Rod's stories about where he was from, how he got the job, and what he'd done in his life.

Rod looked at me one day and told me that most of the guys who come in for a shoeshine don't really try to get to know him like I did. Once, I went to see Rod, and as I greeted him, I had a weird feeling that something wasn't quite right. I walked up to him and said, "Hey, Rod, you all right, buddy? Is everything okay?"

He looked at me and said, "You're unbelievable."

"What do you mean?" I asked.

He said, "You could tell I'm not myself."

After all those years, I liked to think I would know when Rod was okay and when he wasn't. "Is everything all right?" I asked again.

Rod got emotional, and he said, "My wife is really ill. She's in the hospital."

"Oh man, I'm sorry. Is there anything I can do for you to help?"

"No," he said. "My family is in Brazil. The closest person I have in America is my uncle in Florida. I just have to cope the best I can. I'm so glad you came in today. You lifted my spirits."

I told him, "You've got to be strong and pray. Positive thinking is the key."

Sadly, that wasn't enough for Rod's wife. What he experienced was just awful. I stopped by several weeks after our conversation to see how Rod's wife was doing. Sadly, she had passed away. While I was there, he told me, "Tie, that's life. You have to deal with it the best you can. You have no choice." Rod's strength and experiences put everything in perspective. I have no problems compared to what Rod has endured, and he still continues to go through every day with his head held high, doing what he needs to in order to pay the bills. Rod is a shining example of what life is all about and how we should all strive to be.

* * *

My life since I retired has changed dramatically. When I was playing in the NHL, we would fly on planes chartered for the team, so our experience was a little different from the usual lineups at security and boarding gates and the like. When I started travelling after my career, though, I quickly realized just how difficult the job of a Transportation Security Administration staff member is.

One of my favourites is a guy named Charlie Diker. Charlie was among the first people to go through the new TSA training after 9/11, and he did it because his friend and neighbour was one of the firefighters who were trapped and killed in one of the twin towers of the World Trade Center. This poor firefighter had had a wife and two little kids. So when the new TSA training opened up, Charlie took it as soon as possible, wanting to make sure that the tragedy of 9/11 never happened again.

People forget that sort of big-picture thinking. They don't take the time to consider that, when a TSA member is telling them to remove everything from their pockets, to ensure that they have no liquids beyond the acceptable amount, and to take their computers out of bags and briefcases, they aren't saying it because they want to annoy anyone or inconvenience them. That's their job, and they are working diligently to fulfill their role and make sure flights are safe for everyone.

Another great TSA employee is a man named Orin. He's a manager at Newark International Airport, and he helped me to see the importance of the rules. I was once at the airport, and the TSA staff were saying the same things they always do. Well, a lady in front of me could clearly hear their requests, but she decided that the rules didn't apply to her. She had a bottle of water that she wanted to take through security. You know what she told the agents when they found the bottle? "Oh, I just bought that." The agent was very patient with her, and he asked if she'd like to drink the water before she went through security. "Well, that's why I bought it—to drink it!" I couldn't believe how much attitude she was showing over a simple safety concern. Every single day, this kind of stuff goes on at the airport, and every day the good people of the TSA meet people's bad behaviour and bad habits with a positive attitude. It is their job to protect us, day in and day out. The least we can do in return is show them respect by following the rules they set out for us.

One of my favourite people in the travel industry is a nice lady who works at Newark Airport for Porter Airlines. Her name is Elisabeth. She and the head security guy in Newark have no clue about hockey, let alone who I am. A few years ago, neither Elisabeth nor I knew that the other existed. Now Elisabeth wants me to meet her son. I love these people, and I love spending time with them, hearing their stories, and really getting to know them. I see so much of myself in what these people do for a living every day. Any worker, traveller, or person on the street can be pleasant if you're nice to them. How about starting by saying hello with a smile when you pass the gate agent your travel documents? Or making sure that your boarding pass is displayed with your passport open to the right page? Or doing what they tell you to do and not acting like it's so tough? It isn't that hard, and when you get down to it, we all aren't that different.

SHIFT WORK

* * *

At the end of the day, these ideas of talking with everyday people and treating others the way you want to be treated go back to the lessons my parents taught me when I was young. They were big on old school values—beliefs they brought with them from Albania—and they were always trying to make something good out of life. It goes back to skipping school on Fridays so I could help collect the change from my dad's Laundromats in East Detroit. Ever since, I've learned and relearned how to treat everyone equally, no matter what they do for a living or how much they make. I did it when I was a kid, and I still do it to this day.

Yellow cabs are a big part of the landscape in New York; they're how a lot of people get around. Cabdrivers in New York have told me that they need twenty fares between 4:30 a.m. and 4:30 p.m. to make their day's wage. Out of their twenty fares, they will get two bad ones—two really, really rude people. And sometimes, late at night, they'll get drunk people, so you can imagine what that must be like to deal with. The drivers can't stop to eat or use the washroom when they want because they can't park their cars, and they don't have medical coverage or pensions to cover them if something happens. This is the sort of thing they deal with day in and day out. They all ask the same thing—that you just be pleasant when you get in the car. If you do, they'll be nice to you in return. It's a simple thing to do, but it makes a world of difference to them. They can tell right away what a person is like based on the way they acknowledge the driver as they get into the car. They'll know if the passenger wants quiet, or if they want to talk. All they ask is that you say hello, acknowledge them, and be nice to them. It doesn't take much—some kindness and politeness go a long way, no matter where you are in life.

People just need to be recognized, and the people at the top should always remember how important it is to acknowledge everyone who works for them or whom they deal with. I saw it firsthand during my NHL career—winning can be awfully lonely when you do it alone. If you want to be a true leader and a decent person in this world, you have to know the real people who do the hard work in life. That goes for business and everyday life as well as hockey. When I played, I always made a point of knowing the parking lot people, security guards, ice crew, janitors, concession stand people, and maintenance staff at Maple Leaf Gardens and the Air Canada Centre. If everyone would take the time to acknowledge people and get to know them and show them the basic common courtesy they deserve—even just a simple hello and goodbye—the world would be a much better place. Just remember that everyone is equal, on a hockey team and in life. The older I get, the more I have made it my mission in life to remind people of the importance of treating everyone with the respect they deserve. And when I say everyone, I do mean everyone. Because when you get down to it, really, we're all the same.

12

Turning a New Page

A LOT OF athletes and entertainers are people doing what they love and being well compensated for it. But that chapter of their lives doesn't last forever, and they have to keep in mind that, when it ends, they will still have many years ahead of them. The sad fact is that most athletes don't realize that after their careers are over, they will have to work for a living. You're not guaranteed a paycheque anymore. Unless you earn a lot as a player and take care of your money, eventually you'll have to go out and start on a new career. Some people think they will get on a friend's payroll or that companies will just pay them for what they've done, and that they'll somehow be able to maintain the lifestyle they've grown used to. But that just isn't realistic. I have discovered that truly successful people work at what they do all the time, and they never stop. As an athlete and a person, I was always considering the future. There are no rearview mirrors in life. You always have to be looking ahead, not back.

Business was always a part of my life as a hockey player, and I

187

always loved that. After my dad's funeral in the winter of 1991, I kept thinking about his words to me when I broke into the NHL: "What are you going to do if you hurt yourself? You better start learning how to do other things. You have no education." That summer, I decided I would have to get serious about my business career, and from that point on, I never let up. I always pushed myself to try something new—and believe me, I tried a lot of things—or have something on the go other than hockey. This decision served more than one purpose: when I was a young player, the best way I found of dealing with the pressure of fighting was to keep myself busy and to distract my mind during the day leading up to a game.

I started at twenty-three by selling general merchandise and sporting goods to grocery and drugstores. All of the detailed work that went into building those business ventures and relationships—buying goods, making calls, updating spreadsheets—allowed me to focus on something other than fighting before I arrived at the rink. And I was serious about it. I trained myself to be as mentally sharp organizing business deals on days off as I was at nights while I was on the ice. The key to being successful in business is a lot like being a good fighter: the calmer you are, the better. To do what I did, I had to literally play every single game of my career one way: I had to be ready to react and protect my teammates. And to be able to do that, I couldn't afford to obsess about fighting—if I had, I would have driven myself crazy. I wouldn't have been able to sleep, and I wouldn't have been able to play.

The more I taught myself about business, the more I wanted to learn about what it takes to be successful. I used to get teased about wearing a suit and tie to practice. I was the first guy in the NHL with a BlackBerry, and teammates teased me about that, too. Within a year everybody had one. It got to the point where I would be creating spreadsheets in my hotel room while on the road. Teammates would wonder why I bothered with it. But the combination of my dad's words and that need to find ways to deal with the stress of being a fighter in the NHL helped push me forward in my business career. Just as I had to learn how to become a more complete hockey player and not just a fighter, I had to find ways to become a more complete professional, and more than just a hockey player.

* * *

Because I started early, I was able to learn the ins and outs of all different kinds of business. Through more mistakes than successes, I learned that nothing is easy, and eventually I was able to recognize the difference between a good deal and a bad one. That sort of knowledge turned out to be invaluable, and it protected me from investing in bad business deals as a player throughout my career. As my hockey career continued, my networking and the time I spent in the corporate side of the game started to bring me in contact with a range of people in the business world. In the NHL, people are constantly coming into the dressing room to meet the players. And among those people are some very powerful and influential businessmen. A lot of guys couldn't care less about that side of the game; they saw the meet-and-greets as a chore and didn't recognize what an opportunity they were. But I loved them. I spent a lot of time trying to improve myself as a businessman, so to meet those kinds of successful people was perfect. They liked to talk hockey and meet players, and I liked to talk about business and hear their story about how they started out or how they got to where they were. So it turned out to be a win-win.

It was amazing to see how these people came from different walks of life, just like the teammates I'd played with had done. Kenneth Thomson, the late head of the Thomson media empire, used to come into the dressing room at Maple Leaf Gardens. He was not only the richest person in Canada, but one of the richest people on the planet. The first few times I saw him, I didn't really know who he was, but he always came over to have a quick talk. He was as nice and humble as can be. He would quietly compliment me on how hard I played every shift and tell me I had a lot of heart. His words meant a lot to me—here was a man who clearly had an eye for people who worked hard. That clearly served him well. But forget the money; what impressed me most about Mr. Thomson was how he got to our games and how he left: he took the subway. That was a very humbling thing to learn, and it made me appreciate him in a new way.

* * *

It was during the 2004 NHL lockout that I learned how to really take my toughness and apply it off the ice. With negotiations between the owners and the players' union stalling, I figured that our best bet at avoiding a lockout was to bring a small group from both sides together to try and resolve our differences. So I organized a meeting, with Larry Tanenbaum, Leafs board member Dale Lastman, Penguins owner Mario Lemieux, and NHL legal counsel Bill Daly representing the owners and league executives, and Trevor Linden, Ted Saskin, and me representing the players. I felt as though I had a foot in both camps—I was good friends with Mario and Larry, but I was still a player and was represented by Linden and Saskin, then the president and senior director of the NHLPA, respectively.

SHIFT WORK

Our goal was to come up with an agreement that would be deemed acceptable to both Gary Bettman, the commissioner of the NHL, and Bob Goodenow, the executive director of the NHLPA. We hashed things out at Larry's house for a long time, and we had a really productive session. When the meeting finally came to a close, we felt that we had a deal that would work. I drove Mario to the airport right after that, and as he left the car, we high-fived, confident that we had accomplished our goal.

Right after dropping off Mario, I headed back downtown to Harbour Sixty, where I was supposed to meet with the players' representatives so we could present our deal to Goodenow. I walked into the restaurant, and as soon as I saw Bob, I could tell the news wasn't good. I didn't even sit down. I just said, "Well, Bob, I guess you rejected the deal, didn't you?" In the time it had taken me to drive from the airport to the restaurant, all of our work had been tossed out the window. Bob was stubborn, and he had no interest in striking a deal that involved a salary cap. But I was sure that any deal would have to involve one—Larry and Mario had told me as much, and they had no reason to lie to me.

A couple of weeks later, close to seven hundred NHL players— almost every guy in the league—gathered in a hotel in Toronto so that we could hear what our players' association had planned. Partway through presenting his speech, Bob Goodenow suddenly broke from his script.

"So, Tie," he said, "what are your buddies Mario and Larry saying?"

The room went dead quiet. I felt that Bob was challenging me in front of everyone, basically asking if I had a better idea. Everyone turned to look at me as I picked up a microphone to respond.

"What are they saying? They're saying the same thing they've been saying since day one: if there's no salary cap, there's no hockey. You seem to have everybody in this room convinced that there will be a season with no cap. But if you cancel the season and we *do* end up coming back with a salary cap, you and your entire committee better leave the country."

I said my piece, a break in the meeting was called, and I left. Bob Goodenow seemed to think he had become the union, instead of working for it. Of course, what ended up happening? We lost an entire season of salaries, and when we finally did come back to play the next year, it was under a worse agreement than what we'd put together at Larry's house: we would be playing under a salary cap that was $10 million lower than what the owners had agreed to at Larry's; plus, there would be a 24 per cent rollback (effectively a reduction) of player salaries on top of it. Not to mention all of the jobs lost because of the lockout itself. And, five days after the agreement was put into force, Goodenow resigned.

I know business and I know people, and I knew that when the friends I truly trusted in my life, guys like Mario and Larry, told me something, I had no reason to think differently. And I knew that just because someone doesn't want something to be the case—doesn't matter who it is—it doesn't mean they can just look the other way and assume it will go away. Just because someone has an opinion, doesn't mean it's right. We all had to deal with the reality, no matter how much we didn't like it.

* * *

Over the years, some of my business relationships have led to close personal friendships. Or perhaps it might be more accurate to say that my friendships led to closer business relationships. Through my playing career and after, I ended up becoming close friends with people in business like Mark Silver, Mitch Goldhar, Jeff Soffer, Bob Kaiser, Nelson Peltz, and Bill Comrie. Pretty blessed for a guy who never had a lot of formal education and struggled in school with dyslexia. These guys all have a few things in common—they're all family guys, they're all loyal, and they all love sports. But through my friendships with them, I continued to learn about what it takes to make it as a businessman.

But while hockey opened some doors for me in the business world, it was up to me to keep them open and make the relationships work. To continue to learn and succeed, I couldn't just *work* with people—I had to form personal connections with them and bond closely with them, both in business and in life. And sometimes that means taking risks or going outside your comfort zone. Bob Kaiser and I experienced that when we travelled to Russia together.

It was three in the morning, and we were at a nightclub in Moscow with Jeff Soffer and the actor James Caan. This place was wild and a little bit scary, and Jimmy was afraid to go to the bathroom alone. So we went to wait with him, and while Jimmy was waiting in line, a big Russian guy—about six feet, six inches tall—pushed Jimmy aside. He wanted to cut in line. I couldn't believe it!

So I walked up to the Russian, all five feet, ten inches of me, tapped him on the shoulder, and said, "Hey, what are you doing? Don't touch my friend. Show some respect." The Russian just looked at me, then turned to head into the stall.

I couldn't believe how rude this guy was being. So I grabbed his shoulder, turned him back to face me, pulled his face to my level, and said firmly, "Coma. Can you spell *coma*?"

The guy looked confused. "What does that mean?" he asked.

"I'm going to put you in a coma if you don't get out of the way and let my friend go ahead of you."

For a moment, I didn't think it would work. But the Russian actually turned around and went to the back of the line to wait his turn. As we left the club, Jimmy told me he'd never been so scared in his life. Through moments like that, Bob and I share memories and a relationship that you could never form in a boardroom alone.

I had a similar experience with one of my close friends in business and in life, Mark Silver. Mark and I first met when I was traded back to the Leafs from the Jets. We were at a birthday party for a mutual friend, and the party had a 1960s theme. Mark was really into the costume. He was wearing a bright yellow see-through linen shirt with white pants and white shoes. I didn't go quite as far. I was wearing my usual outfit: blue jeans, white T-shirt, and a pair of running shoes. Mark and I got to talking about what the other was wearing, and we've been friends ever since. Through Mark, I've met many other people, including Mitch Goldhar.

Mitch is the guy who got me into squash. He called me one evening and told me to bring my workout clothes to our meeting the next morning. "Are you nuts?" I asked. "I'm not working out—I did that my whole career." But Mitch convinced me, and when I arrived at his office the next day, I was surprised to find that Mitch had a squash court. We walked onto the court, and there was Jonathan Power, the world squash champion. I didn't know Power at the time, but I will never forget the exercise I got that day by running for every ball he sent my way. Of course, while Power barely moved the entire time, I never stopped moving, and I finished the game bent over, gasping for air. That's when Mitch told me, "Until you do it yourself, you don't realize how hard it is to play squash."

I realized it was a lesson I could apply to everything in life—until you try something yourself, you'll never know how hard it is.

Mitch has told me many times that there are different forms of education. He is always reminding me that I'm highly educated when it comes to street smarts and how the world works. Mitch once told me that I have a PhD in life. With me, what you see is what you get. And I guess there is a lot to be said for that. I have always listened to and tried to learn from the people around me. Throughout my life, that was the only way I could find to use my mind to its fullest. For me, it's always been about vision. As a kid, I had to learn to use my memory and my vision to compensate for how hard I found it to concentrate and read in class. On the ice, I had to always have my head on a swivel to watch out for myself and my teammates. And when I entered the business world, I used the experiences from all areas of my life to have a 360-degree view of things.

Mitch taught me how to be shrewd and savvy down to the smallest detail of a project; even the smallest things can help you gain an edge. He and Bill Comrie helped me understand that winning in business is like winning in hockey—you need to have the right team around you, and you need to make sure you always have your sights on the same goal. Just like every player on a team matters, every single experience in life is important—you never know who or what can make a difference.

When it comes to vision, it helps to be able to zero in on what's important. There can often be a lot of distraction or baggage, whether it's on the ice or in a meeting. But if you can focus on the main issue, you can get right to the point and deal with whatever needs to be done. That ability to cut through the noise is important, and one of the best things you can do in order to make things happen is to listen. It sounds simple, but it works. Jeff Soffer put it best when he told me: "I say what I know, and I don't say what I don't know." He's a real networker—I can't count the number of people I've met through Jeff; he's a special friend and very loyal.

My memory is what lets me be so successful at finding synergies and connecting people. Once someone has told me what they're good at or what they do, I can find a way to pair them with a person who complements that. The only hat trick I had in the NHL was the Gordie Howe kind. Now, I have a new kind of hat trick that I use for business: quality, cost effectiveness, and execution. When I see that a person or company has those three things, I know they're people I can deal with. I always loved networking; I like putting people together. I can read people, and I can tell what strengths they have or where they might need help. Everyone needs to be challenged and to get outside their comfort zone, but you have to be careful not to push people out of their depth.

Through all of the experiences I've had—good and bad—I've figured out where my strengths lie. It's similar to the role I had on the ice. In the same way that I protected teammates, I protect my friends and my network now. My loyalty is my bond. I help people find a way to work together, and once you get to know a person as a friend first, it becomes easier to find business partnerships for them. Besides, friendships mean more to me than making money.

Although I know my strengths, I realize that I sometimes have to face my fears. I have never been more scared in my life than when Jeff Soffer took me waterskiing. When I went down to visit Jeff on his boat, I thought we would just have a relaxing time. But before I knew it, I was hanging on behind the boat for dear life. I wasn't trying anything fancy; I was just terrified at the thought of falling in the ocean and having the sharks get me. It freaked me out, and I had no clue what to do. Jeff likes to say I was screaming like a baby. I learned two things from that: 1) I shouldn't stick my nose into something that I know nothing about. And 2), I really don't like sharks.

* * *

As important as it is to find ways to create success, it's just as important to be able to deal with mistakes. How you act in the good times is as meaningful as how you handle the setbacks. It's difficult to learn from our errors, but we have to do it if we're going to overcome them. I found out the hard way that, even when you think you really know someone—and as I said, I believe I am good at reading people—you can still get burned.

I am the stereotypical case of the ex-athlete who almost loses it all after their career is over. I was right there—millions of dollars, a palace of a home, a family around me. I felt like I had everything and that I had my whole life figured out. All of a sudden, like two right hooks, I was hit by a divorce and the financial crisis of 2008. It was the classic double-barrel that brings down so many athletes after they're done playing.

The divorce in 2006 was the first thing to hit, and as it was one of the most publicized divorces in Canadian history, the media storm that came with it was hard to bear. It should never have happened—neither Leanne nor I had wanted to go public, but it happened anyway. There were accusations in the media—a lot of them untrue—and everything just moved so damn fast. Once all of the publicity quieted down, Leanne and I found a way to work together to be the best parents we could while living in separate homes.

Two of my close friends were going through divorces at the same time, so we watched each other's backs and helped each other to get through that difficult time. I was just starting to get sorted out after from my divorce when the 2008 financial crisis hit and everyone thought the world was coming to an end. There are a lot of things in life you can't predict but that happen whether you're ready or not. I didn't expect to get divorced, and I certainly didn't predict the worldwide economic crisis. I lost everything that I had worked so hard for my entire life.

Here's the funny thing about what happened in 2008: through my entire hockey career, I never played the stock market or let any financial guys get close to me. A lot of them tried—each one told me that they had a better deal than what the last person offered. They either wanted my money, or to use my profile to raise funds for their own gain. I got a taste of how that could go wrong when I was a young player.

When I was twenty-three years old, I was introduced to an investor through a restaurant owner who was a friend of mine. At least, I *thought* he was an investment banker. The first time I met him, my gut feeling was not good. But I trusted my friend, and, against my better judgment, I invested some of my hard-earned money with the guy. That turned out to be my first mistake. I went to visit the guy a little while later to ask about my money, and when I showed up at the address he gave me, I waited in the driveway for him to come home. He didn't show for a long time, so eventually I just walked into the house. I knew I was in trouble when I saw that the house had no furniture in it. I never saw the guy or any of the money I had given to him. After learning that powerful lesson at only twenty-three, I told myself I'd never again trust anyone with my money.

SHIFT WORK

After I retired, I suddenly found myself with new friends who worked on Bay Street. Some friends. I should have clued in from the beginning. I was being taken out to expensive meals and flown to meetings on private planes all over the world, and although I always tried to pay my own way, everything would be covered with a company credit card or expense account. I was amazed at the money these guys would throw around. I should have been cautious and taken more time after I retired to navigate the crowd to find out whom I could trust. But what did I do instead? I started letting guys sell me on shady stocks, funds, and all the same kind of garbage that burned so many other people in 2008. And what happened when the crisis hit and people's true colours started coming out? Those guys were suddenly nowhere to be found.

If that experience taught me anything, it was that, no matter what anyone says to you or does for you, nothing is a guarantee. Somebody told me once that success is relative: the more success, the more relatives. When friends need help—financially or in any other way—I never thought twice about helping them out. A lot of people, when they need you, claim to be your best friend. My dad did a lot for the people around him, and he never expected anything from them in return. He just did it out of the goodness of his heart. I am the same way, but you would think I would have learned from his mistakes. Well, I did and I didn't. I ended up helping all kinds of people, but most of those deals weren't on paper. Like my dad, I have always been the kind of guy to do things on a handshake. I've learned that those days are mostly gone now. But at the end of the day, I did give certain people opportunities. And a lot of people took me for granted because of who I was. They thought my time was meant entirely for fun and games, that they could always turn to me for whatever they wanted. Well, when all of a sudden the roles were reversed and it was me who needed help, I got to see who my real friends were. If you're a real person, you're a real friend, through thick and thin. People used me for my relationships; or at least, they tried to. As they tried, I cut them off. As soon as I sensed they were trying to use me, we were done.

No matter how bad my financial troubles seemed, I tried my best to keep things together. Sometimes, I had to turn to people for help, and luckily, I had some true friends and family around me that I could trust and rely on. I'm old school. It goes back to the values my parents taught me: if you hit a rough patch, you think positively and remember that you have to help yourself before others can help you. If you keep your head down and work hard, you can get through just about anything. But for the times that you can't, or when you're not able to do it all yourself, you should never be afraid to ask for help. I learned that eventually, and it was those lessons my family taught me as a young man that held me together.

Looking to the example my dad had set for us, I made sure never to let my kids know what I was going through in those difficult financial times. I had an obligation to my children. No matter how bad things were, I refused to let my divorce or my financial difficulties change the lives of my kids. That wasn't easy to do when I had to walk around in the spotlight with my every decision tracked and criticized; I'll always be proud of how the kids handled that. There was no way I was going to sacrifice their futures or their education, no matter how much debt I was in. I saw it as my responsibility to make sure that my kids' lives didn't change as a result of my difficulties.

Leanne and I had always agreed that the kids came first. For the first five years after the divorce, I still had a key to Leanne's house so that I could be a better help in raising the kids. Leanne is an incredible mother, and though we might have been divorced, neither of us ever stopped being active in parenting. We tried to keep life as normal as possible. Some of my favourite moments with my kids in that time were the quiet ones driving them to school or picking them up. Neither of us wanted to take our kids away from the lives and opportunities that they had been given. It helped that I had support from caring people. My sister, Trish, and her husband, Ori, were like second parents to my kids; I don't know what I would have done without them. And Nelson and Claudia Peltz were a big support and inspiration to me as they mentored me in what it takes to be a good parent. They have eight kids, and they are so open with each and every one of them. Their lives had been incredibly challenging at some points. Their son, Brad, is like a younger brother to me. When I was going through those tough times in 2008, Brad was still a young guy playing hockey at Yale. Unfortunately, he was also going through similar troubles to what I had with someone who was in a position of power over him. Brad's dream was to play in the NHL, but his career was being derailed before it even got started. I don't know how he did it, but Brad managed to stay positive through that whole experience. It put things in perspective for me. I realized how lucky I was to have had a full career, and Brad's strength and his parents' advice inspired me to believe that there was a light at the end of the tunnel. Nelson once told me, "There's no guarantee in life that if you work hard you will succeed. But if you don't work hard, I can guarantee you that you will fail." So I made sure I held up my end of the bargain, and I went out and worked my butt off to make sure the kids were able to enjoy the same lives and lifestyle they had before the tough times hit. I refused to let my burdens fall on their shoulders.

I reached the lowest point the day I came home to find an eviction notice on my front door. After my divorce, I'd moved into an apartment, and I had grown attached to the people—like Nigel—who worked there. I was upset because I was only a few days late on my rent, and, as with the problems I'd had at the end of my career, I found myself struggling to find a way to control things. Only people who have found such signs on their doors will know how it feels, how deep the pit in the bottom of your stomach drops when you're told you're going to lose your home—it's a situation I never want to find myself in again. It was worse than anything I'd experienced before any fight. But sitting alone in my apartment that night, I suddenly became inspired. I told myself that my situation wasn't right, and so I had to find a way to fix it. I wasn't going to be getting any handouts, and there wasn't anyone coming on a white horse to save me. I would have to earn everything back. I had made mistakes, and now it was up to me to make sure that I fulfilled my obligations, not only to my kids and Leanne, but also to myself.

Whether it was the divorce or the money, I could only blame myself for everything. It was times like that when the lessons I learned in the dressing room and on the streets came through to save me in the real world. I not only wanted to survive; I wanted to succeed. I was determined, and I knew that my family still came first. So I didn't just lie there and feel sorry for myself. I couldn't wait for someone to turn my life around for me. I did whatever was needed, simply because it had to be done. I put my head down and plowed through.

Just like my dad, I didn't expect anything from anybody. There is no question that I had to work hard. I focused on my consulting career, and from the time I got up until the time I finally went to bed, my phone would be constantly ringing with calls, e-mails, and text messages from people across different time zones. There were businessmen out there who were more educated than I was, but I made sure that no one outworked me. Eventually, through hard work and sacrifice, I was able to get my head above water and slowly start to recover. No matter how bad it looks, if you apply yourself and keep a positive attitude, you can make anything happen.

One thing is for sure: I don't have all my eggs in one basket anymore. I've learned from my mistakes, and I rely more and more on what I have built up my whole life: my reputation. I make sure that I only involve myself with businesses and people if I know I can trust their word. Above all, I aim to never embarrass myself again.

During my playing career, guys used to laugh at me for being involved in business. They got a real kick out of making fun of me. But all that teasing was worth it. Because if I hadn't been laying the groundwork for my business career for years before I retired from the NHL, I would never have been able to survive what happened to me after I retired. I would have just ended up as a statistic—another ex-athlete who lost it all. Now I'm at the stage of my life where I would just be a fool if I had let what happened to me in 2008 happen again. Like I said, my dad always held his cards tight to his chest, and it's taken me a while, but I've learned to do the same. I am not ashamed to admit that it took a long time for me to finally learn how the world turns. I learned the hard way to stick to what I know best. My dad died when I was still a young man, but in a lot of ways, he continues to watch over me. He told me years ago I needed to learn how to do things besides playing hockey. Well, for better or for worse, I did, and I like to think my dad would be proud to see how my career and life have grown over the years. And, more important, he'd be so happy to see how my kids have done the same. You always have to remember that you have the rest of your life to live; don't just live for today. Enjoy every day, but always keep your eyes open and your guard up to protect yourself, your family, and your future. After my struggles in 2008, Mitch Goldhar told me, "Put your head down, and build your walls high." Well, after what happened in 2008, the walls around me and my family are higher than ever.

13

Family

I WOULD DO anything for my kids. I have a son, Max, and two daughters, Carlin and Avery, and they mean the world to me. I would do or sacrifice anything to take care of them. Each one of my kids is different in their own way, and all three impress me every day. I have been blessed with a few things in my life, but seeing how all three of my kids have turned out means more to me than everything else.

Hockey seems to run in the family. When I first entered the NHL, my brother, my cousins, and I would never let a teammate or hockey player close to any girls in the family. They knew how protective I was. But if you were to ever meet Adam Graves, you'd know why he was the exception to that rule. The first time that Gravey met my cousin Violet, I had no idea that he liked her. I should have clued in—after he met her, he couldn't stop talking about her. In the spring of 1991, he and I drove back to Ontario together in his Bronco SUV. Sure enough, while he was dropping me off, Gravey asked if he could get Violet's phone number so he could take her out to dinner and a show. Fast-forward to years later, and there I was, on my way to the high school graduation of their daughter, Madison—my goddaughter. She was the valedictorian, and Leanne had asked me to stop on my way over to pick up flowers for her. By the time I got to the event, everyone was already seated, and I had to walk to the front of the room carrying a huge bouquet of flowers. Madison's speech was amazing. I cried so much all the way through it because she touched on every value that is important to our family. She brought the roof down.

When Max was young, he referred to hockey as "daddy's work." I would bring him to Maple Leaf Gardens and the ACC a lot when he was a kid. On the way in, we'd stop to hug Senidu, the parking lot attendant at the ACC, and then we'd high-five the security guards and mess around with the ice crew and ushers. Max would stay on the ice for hours, and when we'd leave, he would cry most of the way home because he didn't want to leave. Right from day one, it was clear that Max loved being on the ice and playing hockey. I never had to push him—he came into it all on his own, and he couldn't get enough of it. One look at Max on the ice as a kid, and you just knew how much he loved it. Since Mario and Mats were my closest hockey friends, they were around Max so often that he came to think of them as his uncles.

When Max was twelve years old, he was diagnosed as a type 1 diabetic. Leanne and I were in the room with Max as he heard the news. We weren't sure how he would react, but the first words out of his mouth were, "Can I still play hockey?"

The doctor, Dr. Perlman—a tiny, energetic guy—got right in Max's face. At twelve, Max was already the same size as Dr. Perlman.

"Can you play hockey? Do you know who Bobby Clarke is?

He's the toughest darn hockey player there was. And he was a diabetic."

Later, as we were driving home from the hospital, Max asked me if I knew who Bobby Clarke was. I didn't mention to him then about how, as a kid about Max's age, I had knocked out my front teeth to look more like Clarke.

"Of course I know who Bobby Clarke is. He was one of my favourites as a kid."

"What number did he wear?"

"Sixteen."

Max paused and thought for a second. "Do you think Mats would mind if I changed my jersey number from thirteen to sixteen?" he asked.

I smiled as I told him that Mats wouldn't mind at all.

* * *

Max is a special hockey player. He's been an elite-level player since he was young, and because of that, he has been forced to grow up a lot quicker than other kids his age. As a hockey dad—or anyone's parent, for that matter—one of your goals is to get your kid into good habits. So when Max was young, I did whatever I could to help him in his hockey career. If he asked me anything—about life or hockey—I told him what I thought. He may not always have liked what I had to say, but that never stopped him from asking.

It takes a ton of commitment to be a professional athlete or an entertainer. If you want it badly enough, you can make it. But you have to be willing to sacrifice things in your life to get there, and you need to be all in, now more than ever. It's the only way. You also have to be able to deal with adversity and be mentally tough.

There's no fast track. One of the most important things for anyone who goes into those careers is to have an education. Everyone is different, and from day one, Leanne and I knew that Max was special. We knew he'd be able to make whatever move he wanted. So when Max chose to play junior rather than go to college, Leanne and I had no choice but to support him, even though we felt differently. If he weren't as talented an athlete as he was—if he had been an average player who wasn't ready or who wasn't physically or mentally strong enough—then it might have been a little different. But we knew Max would be ready to join the junior ranks as a sixteen-year-old. And he was.

The day I first dropped Max off in London to play for the Knights, I told him, "Now I'm just your dad. I'm here to encourage you and be a positive voice for you. I'm not going to be *that* kind of dad." I wasn't going to tell Max what to do or dictate his life. I wanted to use my experience to guide him, but I also knew he had to figure things out for himself. There's a lot of me in Max, but he's his own person. He is smart, and I knew he could make up his own mind. I left it to him to find his way. People would whisper that I had influence over where he played, but that isn't true at all. I'll always be there for Max, but his decisions are his own.

I gave Max his space after he joined the Knights. But I was always ready to step in and show him positive support if he needed it. The time when I could feel that Max needed me the most was after he was left off Canada's World Junior team in December 2013. As a kid, Max had always been glued to the TV during the World Junior Championship. It was his dream to play on that team, and I knew he would be upset after he didn't make it. So I wasn't surprised when, after the team was announced and he wasn't on it, Max reached out to me for the first time since he had started playing with the Knights. I was in New York at the time, and I jumped on a plane to head to London right away. I had to help Max realize that, even if he didn't agree with or understand the decision, he had a choice to make. I told him that in situations like this, you are able to do one, and only one, thing: control what you do. Max concentrated on that, and in the weeks following the World Junior Championship, he showed Team Canada what they'd missed by leaving him off the team.

Because Max is both diabetic and celiac, he constantly has to watch his diet. But no matter how hard Max tries to do all the right things, he is still human, and sometimes he gets sick. What impresses me, though, is that he never complains about anything and always wants to go out there and play through whatever he's experiencing. That's what successful leaders do, and that's the kind of thing that makes me proud of him.

Once, when Max was competing in the Canada-Russia Subway Super Series, he started to feel sick just before the tournament began. He was scheduled to play five games in five nights, which was asking too much considering he was so ill. But Max didn't want to let anybody down—not Knights general manager Mark Hunter, not the team, and not the Super Series organizers. I know my son, and I knew that Max would try to play no matter what anyone else said. During the first game of the series on the Thursday night, Max was so sick that he lost eight pounds. From there, he played games with the Knights on Friday, Saturday, and Sunday, and then again in the Subway Series on Monday. He just refused to sit back.

But it isn't all about hockey with Max. He's a young man who makes me proud in how he carries himself and how well he treats everyone around him. I was once in London to see a Knights game during Max's first year with the team when Dave, one of the security guys at the arena, pulled me aside. He told me that in the twelve years he had been working security, Max was the first kid to come up and introduce himself. Max had gone up to Dave and said, "Hi, I'm Max Domi, and I'm going to play for the London Knights. And your name, sir, is?" Dave had been a little taken aback by this, and after he told Max his name, Max said, "It's a pleasure to know you, sir." They'd talked a bit, and then Max had made his way over to the rest of the team. Believe me, hearing what Max said means as much to me as it did to Dave.

Max has always shown that sort of sincerity and humility. At the 2015 Conn Smythe sports dinner, Max was invited to attend as one of their sports celebrities. I got to the dinner just in time to hear him speak, and his words brought tears to my eyes. In one interview that Max did that night, he stopped after a question to pay tribute to two children from the Easter Seals charity who were in attendance. I was touched to see that, even at a celebrity event, Max was putting those kids and their charity ahead of himself. And he was figuring it out standing on his own two feet. Afterwards, a number of people—including Paul Henderson, Pinball Clemons, and Gregg Zaun—came up to me to say that they thought Max was a special kid. It made me consider how proud my dad would have been to see Max at that moment.

* * *

Each of my kids is so unique and special in their own way. My daughter Carlin is incredibly compassionate, and she helps bring the family together. When Carlin moved to London to attend the University of Western Ontario, she asked all of us to move her there and help set her room up. At Western, when you pull in for your first day of school, you get a certain time slot and current students help the arriving students to move everything into their rooms. Volunteers at the residence take all the stuff out of the parents' trunk, and everybody forms an assembly line to pass stuff up the stairs all the way to the kid's room. It's a cool experience, especially for someone who never made it past high school. Carlin had told me to be at the dorm at a certain time, and as she finished describing the plan, she said, "Dad, whatever you do, don't wear a hat and glasses when you get there. It only draws more attention to you."

So I showed up, without a hat, glasses, or anything else to hide my face. I pulled up and got out of the car, and as I walked into the dorm, people started to recognize me and began asking me for pictures. Soon, it wasn't just the new students and their families who were gathering around, but also the volunteers and movers. At this point, I just wanted to find my family. So I called Carlin and asked, "Carlin, where are you?"

"Where are *you*?" she responded.

When I told her, she said, "Dad, you're at the wrong dorm!"

When I finally got to the right place, Carlin, Avery, and Leanne weren't finished setting up yet, but Carlin said, "Dad, we're not done yet. Just go and watch Max's practice and come back when he's done."

When I got back from Max's practice, I decided I didn't want to go through what had happened the first time I pulled up. So I put on a hat and glasses, and I snuck up the stairs to Carlin's room. There were people on every step, passing boxes up the stairs, and every time I passed them, I would look at the wall to try to hide my face. Still, halfway up the stairs, I heard someone say, "That's Tie Domi!" I sped up the stairs to Carlin's room, and as I closed the door, I admitted, "I don't think your plan worked." Carlin wasn't too happy. She looked out her door and saw that the hallway and stairwell were packed with people looking at her room.

"Dad!" Carlin exclaimed.

Carlin, Avery, and Leanne didn't want to have anything to do with the group in the hallway, so they bolted out the door and down the stairs. I walked out of the room last, and the whole floor was quiet. The closest group was a bunch of kids who looked like hockey players or some sort of athlete. I talked with them for a bit, and then I turned serious. I pulled out a handmade sign that I had taken off the wall on the stairwell that referenced Carlin's dorm. It turns out that students called her residence, Saugeen-Maitland Hall, "the Zoo" because it was known as the biggest party place at Western. The sign said, "Saugeen fathers, thank you for your yummy daughters."

"Did you boys see this?" I asked. "Were you the ones who made this?"

They all shook their heads so hard I thought they were going to fall off. You should have seen their faces—it was like they'd seen a ghost.

I said to them, "Now that you all know where my daughter lives, I want you to remember something. I am going to be coming around here every weekend because my son, Max, plays for the London Knights. So I will be here every weekend. And I want you *all* to be able to look me in the eye every time I see you. I know you know where my daughter lives. So I know you guys will be looking out for her now, *right*?"

This one guy—the smallest kid in the crew—put his hand up, and you could tell he was a sweet kid.

"Mr. Domi?" he said.

214

"You can call me Tie."

"Tie, if there is one person on this earth I don't want to piss off, it's you."

After that first year at university, Carlin told me she wanted to live with my sister at their cottage for the summer. I said, "Carlin, you're not going up there and living like a queen." Leanne and I made a deal with Carlin that if she could get a job that would bring her some life experience, she could live up there for the summer. Sure enough, she got a job at Rocky Crest Golf Club driving the beverage cart. I thought it was great—she would gain valuable life experience dealing with different people. My kids might not be able to learn the street skills that I had, but that's not a bad thing. They've all still found a way to learn the valuable lesson of how to deal with people.

Later that summer, I went up north to have a day with Carlin. I got up there on a Friday and met her for dinner. The next morning, I woke up to find a note from her saying that she'd reserved me a lunch spot at the golf course. As I was sitting on the patio looking over the beautiful eighteenth hole, all of a sudden a girl came up to me and said, "Mr. Domi, I just wanted to tell you that your daughter Carlin, well, she's our leader, and she's the nicest person. She smiles every day, and she is so easy to talk to."

I had barely said thank you when the assistant general manager, who had worked there for four years, came up and said, "Tie, your daughter lights up the room every day that she's here. She's supposed to be done at a certain time every day, but she always stays longer and she never complains. She's the first one to fill in if someone needs it."

Finally, the managers, a husband and wife, came up and summed it up for me: "Tie, your daughter is the best girl who's ever worked for us." I was crying the whole time these people were talking to me; luckily, I had sunglasses on. When others say such amazing things about your kids like that, it's the ultimate compliment.

* * *

My youngest daughter, Avery, is a real firecracker. She is smart, polite, a great basketball and volleyball player, and she isn't shy about putting me in my place. As a teenager, she is also obsessed with her iPhone. When I'm trying to talk with her, I might as well video-call her so that my face is on the screen of her phone, because that's all she seems to look at. Like most kids now, sometimes it can seem like she isn't listening to anything I say. But, as I discovered, she is listening and learning all the time.

I'm not a cottage or a camp person. And unlike a lot of parents, I wasn't usually one for sending my kids to summer camp. I always thought that one week at camp, tops, was more than enough time to be away. But in the summer of 2014, Avery went to a leadership camp. I was going to see her on the last day of camp, and she called me during her week there to tell me she was having the time of her life. She said, "Dad, the leader of the camp keeps asking me questions about the examples because he knows I've already learned them from you." As a teenager, Avery was already living the lessons that others were just learning for the first time. When I went to pick Avery up, I heard even more great things about her from her counsellors. They all complimented Avery on her leadership skills, how pleasant she is, and her manners.

At Avery's school, there is an award given out each year in memory of a young girl, Emma Federer, who, sadly, passed away a few years ago. Each year, students submit proposals for a project that focuses on supporting the school's athletics, improving school spirit, or giving back to the community. The award, called Emma's Gift, is given to the students with the winning proposal so that they can create their event. The first year that the award was given out, Carlin—who was close with Emma—and three of her friends were the recipients, and they put together a fashion show. And three years later, Avery received the same award as she and two of her friends organized a charity run—Emma's Colour Run—for the school.

Nothing makes a parent prouder than hearing positive things about their kids and seeing them use their talents in such incredible ways to help others. Believe me, I can relate to all those parents out there who wonder if their kids are ever listening to them, because I live it every day. I have three kids who live on their phones. And when I do get ahold of them with a text message, all I get back is a "k" or "yes," and that's it. That's the new world. But forget the technology or what I think is right. Nowadays, people assume that kids pay more attention to Instagram, Snapchat, and Facebook than the people around them. I can be sitting with my kids and, although they're physically there, they're more in touch with countless other people across social media. So how do I get my message across? I say it loudly. I've learned that, even if your kids are staring at their phones, you always have to keep talking to them, because no matter what you might think, they're always listening. Avery showed me that. I should have realized that she was always listening and learning. She was just doing it her own way; she was finding her own way to live the values I've tried to teach her.

*   *   *

It is fascinating to watch kids figure out their lives and go through experiences in different ways. As parents, we try to guide and protect them, but at the end of the day, it's up to them to find their own way. You hope that they won't take the kinds of falls you did. But when they do have setbacks, you are there to help them, whether it's a difficult decision or an easy one. My kids know that their mother and I will always be there for them.

It turns out that each of my kids has always listened and learned to be aware of real-life experiences. I've made a lot of mistakes over the years, but it turns out that, after years of watching and listening to me, all three of my kids learned a few things. Max, Carlin, and Avery have all turned out better than I could have ever hoped for. Some people tell me I have sacrificed a lot for my kids. I don't see it that way. When you love someone as much as I love my kids, it is never a sacrifice. It is just what you do. It's something my dad and mom taught me growing up: your kids always come first.

As a hockey player, I left behind a record that included having the most fights in NHL history, being a leader, and giving it my all every shift. But Max, Carlin, and Avery are the true legacy that I'll leave behind.

CONCLUSION

'M FINISHING this book just a few months after Team Canada won the 2015 World Junior Championship. That was a special event for our family. After being left off the team in 2014, Max had earned a spot on the roster, and the games took place in Toronto and Montreal, so I was going to be able to attend all of them with my daughters, Leanne, and my girlfriend, Heather. My whole family would be gathered together, ready to enjoy what came, win or lose.

There was an incredible atmosphere around the World Juniors. Interest was high, both in the host cities and across the country. After Canada beat the USA in Montreal, the fans chanted Max's name, and then an incredible 7.1 million viewers tuned in to the final game, in which Team Canada faced Russia in a bid to end a five-year gold medal drought.

It made me so happy to see Max entering the next stage of his life, which he had dreamed of for so long and worked so hard to reach. I knew that my job now wasn't to protect him or insert myself into everything he did. It was Max's turn to take the spotlight. So, during the tournament, I stuck to doing what every parent would do for their child: I dropped off dinners for Max at his hotel, went to the games with my daughters, and gave everyone the space they needed to make their mark. Over those three weeks, as Canada made its way towards a gold medal, the country—and the world—finally got to see what I'd known Max could do his entire life. He was succeeding on one of the biggest stages in the hockey world, and he was doing it all while staying humble and true to himself. The bigger the stage and the better he played, the more modest Max became. It got to the point that he started being criticized for being too humble!

But none of it got to him. He never took a shift off, and he did it with his family and team around him every step of the way. In what my kids are able to accomplish and how they act—together and by themselves—I see that the lessons and values my parents taught me are alive and well.

In the gold medal game, Max rose to the occasion. He'd always loved the pressure, ever since he was a kid. The game was intense, and it was close right to the very end. But when the final buzzer sounded, it was Canada that came out on top, beating Russia 5–4. The crowd at the Air Canada Centre was deafening as the Canadian players mobbed each other in celebration. Finally, the teams lined up for the awards ceremony. After the medals had been given out, the MVPs were announced, and words can't describe how proud I was of Max when he was named the most valuable forward in the tournament. The fans loved it, too, and as Max accepted the award with his gold medal around his neck, the crowd started chanting his name.

I watched Max wave to the tens of thousands of people as their chants got louder and louder, and as I sat back and looked down at my daughters' smiling faces, I felt my shift was done.

ACKNOWLEDGMENTS

I'D LIKE to thank Jim Lang for doing all the research and interviews with my friends and family for the book, and for translating my thoughts to the page. I hope you had fun, and thank you for all the time you had to spend away from your family while working on the book.

To all of my friends: Thank you for taking the time and sharing your stories, many of which I'm sure we couldn't publish. I love you all.

Thanks to Allen Fleishman for making this book happen.

Thank you to Kevin Hanson, David Millar, Brendan May, and all of the staff at Simon & Schuster. I'm glad things turned out the way they did. It's been a long, interesting process, but I'm glad I did it.

To everyone who I talk about in this book, thank you. Without you, this book never could have happened.

Thank you to all of my family. My sister, Trish, is the family historian and provided many of the stories and photos in the book.

ACKNOWLEDGMENTS

Leanne helped me do and be so much, as both a hockey player and a father. The support of my girlfriend, Heather, throughout the whole process of writing this book has been incredible. And my children, Carlin, Max, and Avery, are what keep me going.

Finally, to the reader, I hope you enjoyed the book.

—TD

To say this book project was a "team effort" is the ultimate understatement. Tie made a name for himself during his NHL career as the ultimate team player, so it is only natural that his belief in teamwork stayed with us throughout the writing of this book. There are many people who made this book possible, and I want to make sure to acknowledge all of them.

First of all, I would like to thank my agent Brian Wood for his dogged determination in bringing all the parties together to make this complicated project possible.

Next up, I need to give special thanks to the crew at Simon & Schuster: Publisher Kevin "Messier" Hanson, David Millar, and my invaluable editor, Brendan May. I will be forever grateful for Kevin and his staff for their undying support and faith in me as we researched and wrote the book.

Without question, my wife Patricia and my daughters, Adriana and Cassandra, deserve special praise for showing unbelievable patience and understanding in the year it took to research and write this book. At one point my wife noted I was spending more time with Tie than with her. Eventually she would ask me, "How's your bromance going?"

I definitely need to thank the staff and management at my radio station, 105.9 The Region, for being extremely accommodating and understanding during the writing of this book.

224

ACKNOWLEDGMENTS

There is no way this book would have been written without the help of a number of outstanding websites. They include: hockeyfights .com, hockeydb.com, hockeyreference.com, thn.com (*The Hockey News*), NHL.com, ontariohockeyleague.com, and YouTube.com.

The first thing you realize when you are part of a book project that involves Tie Domi is that he has a staggering circle of family and friends.

From hockey to business and all points in between, Tie seems to know everyone, and they are all friends with him. Usually one text or email was all it took to get a response from someone in researching the book. Everyone I spoke with mentioned that Tie was the kind of friend that would do anything for you. After speaking to his friends, I get the impression they would do the exact same for him.

I greatly enjoyed speaking with Tie's brother, Dash, and sister, Trish. Tie's sister Trish is the official family historian and was an invaluable asset during the research and writing of this book.

A stick tap goes out to Burton Lee and the entire Peterborough Petes organization for all of their efforts.

From Tie's days with the New York Rangers, I would like to thank Mark Messier, Adam Graves, and Joe Cirella for taking time to speak with me. Graves in particular is, as advertised, possibly the nicest hockey player I ever met.

Speaking of the Rangers, Michael Rappaport from their media relations department deserves a big pat on the back for all of his help researching the details of Tie's years in New York.

I also need to thank a number of former players for taking time to tell me about their memories of Tie. They include Ken Daneyko, Marty McSorley, Jason Woolley, and Keith Primeau.

Tie's Maple Leafs teammates were extremely generous with

ACKNOWLEDGMENTS

their time. Mats Sundin, Bryan McCabe, Darby Hendrickson, Cory Cross, and Glenn Healy all went out of their way to speak with me. McCabe is also one of the funniest storytellers you will ever meet.

One of Tie's best friends during his playing days in Toronto was long-time assistant equipment manager Scott McKay. Scotty is not only a great interviewee, he is a prime example of all that is good about the NHL.

I was constantly blown away at the all-stars of the business world who call Tie their friend. All of the men I spoke with — Bill Comrie, Brad Nelson, Jeff Soffer, Mitchell Goldhar, Mark Silver, and Robert Kaiser — are extremely successful in their own right and all of them were a pleasure to deal with.

Spending so much time with Tie allowed me the privilege of meeting so many different personalities. Tie's circle of friends extends far beyond the world of hockey and business. While none of them are household names, they are all amazing in their own right.

There was Rod the shoeshine guy at the Waldorf Astoria in New York. What an amazingly resilient man.

There was also Milton the head server and Joe the doorman at the Four Seasons hotel in New York. Joe is what you would call a real "stand-up" guy and Milton is the most positive human being you will ever meet.

In addition, there was the staff at Tie's favourite coffee shops in Yorkville in Toronto and in SoHo in New York. Meeting Tie's buddy Mario at his favourite New York coffee shop was a real treat (positive mental attitude, baby).

From there you have Tie's long-time hairdresser in Toronto, Santino, the security staff at the Budweiser Gardens in London, the security staff and parking lot attendants at Air Canada Centre, Nigel

ACKNOWLEDGMENTS

and the concierge staff at Tie's apartment in Toronto, and the staff at Elleven Restaurant in Toronto (they really do make a great kosher hotdog).

During the writing of the book I was able to spend some invaluable time with the true "godfather" of Toronto, Ted Nikolaou. Ted owns the Harbour Sixty Steakhouse near Air Canada Centre and, like the man, his entire staff is first class all the way.

And last, but certainly not least, the person I owe the most thanks to is Tie Domi.

Like anyone else who reads this book, I thought I knew Tie and what he was all about. But during all of the time it took to put this book together, I realized that the real Tie Domi is far more complex than the one that hockey fans watched every night during his lengthy NHL career. I will be forever grateful to Tie for agreeing to do this book. By doing so, it allowed me entry into a rare world that is usually only reserved for those who play the game at the NHL level. Tie has lived a pretty incredible life, and to have him recount it all to me was an amazing experience.

But here is what you have to know about Tie Domi: When you look past his tough-guy persona and his 333 NHL fighting majors, you will find a decent human being who would do anything for his kids, his family, and his friends. Tie Domi is definitely a one-of-a-kind personality that just doesn't come around very often. Here's to the next chapters in his amazing life.

—JL